Sir Thomas Malory

A BIOGRAPHY

In a north window of the Church,

Orate pro Iohī Malorey, et philippa vrore eius.

SIR THOMAS MALORY'S PARENTS.

(Dugdale's "Antiquities of Warwickshire": The stained glass window
formerly in Grendon Church.)

THE MALORY COAT-OF-ARMS.

(From Harleian MS. 1404, fo. 62.)

Sir Thomas Malory

HIS TURBULENT CAREER

A Biography by

EDWARD HICKS

1970

OCTAGON BOOKS

New York

Reprinted 1970
by special arrangement with Harvard University Press

OCTAGON BOOKS
A DIVISION OF FARRAR, STRAUS & GIROUX, INC.
19 Union Square West
New York, N. Y. 10003

LIBRARY OF CONGRESS CATALOG CARD NUMBER: 78-120630

TO THE MEMORY OF

𝔐𝔶 𝔚𝔦𝔣𝔢

WHO, DESPITE HER ILL-HEALTH, WAS
KEENLY INTERESTED IN THE PROGRESS
OF MY MALORY RESEARCHES

Preface

En habes, lector benevole. — Here you may find, gentle reader, a multitude of exciting novelties about that Sir Thomas Malory of Newbold Revel and Winwick whom I had the good luck to identify, thirty odd years ago, with the author of *Le Morte d'Arthur.* Such a feast needs no proclaiming; but, since Mr. Hicks has done me the honour to request me to write a note of invitation, I must try to do what he asks as unobtrusively as I can.

To hard-headed and stout-hearted students of literary antiquities the important facts which our keen and indefatigable investigator has discovered will make instant appeal. Nor will they be shocked or disconcerted by the wildness of the actions recorded. To the sentimental reader we may leave the task of adjusting Sir Thomas's biography, as now revealed, to the notions he may have derived of him from his immortal romance. Everybody must admire the way in which Mr. Hicks has gathered such a wealth of pertinent information, historical and social, to set forth in a true light the extraordinary conditions which made Malory's career natural and normal in fifteenth-century England. As Pike, the historian of crime, remarked long ago: "The qualities of the knight errant and the gentleman have often been attributed to the highwayman and the brigand. Nor can it be disputed that the highwayman and the brigand have much in common with the knight errant."

Let us not be over-much concerned by the charges brought against Sir Thomas Malory in 1451, serious as they may appear in the light of modern manners. "Possession by the strong arm had for so many centuries constituted the best title to land that the best legal claim to it was almost valueless until practically asserted by setting foot on the soil." The statute against forcible entry was not passed until the fifth year of Richard II, and the old custom long survived the enactment, yielding only to what we are prone to call the Tudor Despotism. A logical corollary to this rough-and-ready method of asserting title was the practice of seizing for one's self money or other personal property to which one laid claim. Such riots were of daily occurrence, and carried no stigma of social disgrace, whatever the law might have to say to them if they got into court, as most of them did not. Besides, an indictment is merely an accusation; it is not evidence: and the lawyers, as we know, had a way of including in such a document everything that the prosecution could think of, and far more than anybody expected to prove. Now Mr. Hicks, the discoverer of this extraordinarily interesting record and of other entries referring to the same case, has not succeeded in finding any account of a trial. For aught we know, then, Malory was acquitted on all the counts. Anyhow, there is no probability that he was convicted on all of them, or that, if convicted, he was punished by imprisonment. At worst, he had to make restitution and pay a substantial fine. The double charge of rape was manifestly absurd — a mere legal formula if the woman of the house was present and had been forcibly removed from her dwelling while it was ransacked. Nor is there any likelihood that Malory had lain in wait to kill Buckingham, though he may have been in Coombe woods while the duke was a guest at the

Abbey. What makes it clear that he was either not convicted, or not punished by imprisonment, is the fact that on March 26, 1453, Duke Humphrey and others were commissioned to arrest him again on what appear to be new charges. Nor did this new prosecution, it seems, result in the penalty of imprisonment. He had the King's pardon for all offences committed before July 9, 1455. Fresh offences, however, seem to have resulted in Malory's continuous, or almost continuous, imprisonment for three years, from 1457 to 1460. That he was in confinement when he penned his valediction in 9 Edward IV (at some time between March 4, 1469, and March 3, 1470) may be regarded as certain. Perhaps he was still in prison when he died on the 14th of the following March. But I see no evidence that he had been confined for any considerable period between 1460 and 1469. His exclusion from the general pardon of 1468 was probably due to some political offence; for almost all of the persons associated with him in this exclusion were involved, or thought to be involved, in recent Lancastrian plots.

But enough! I have yielded to the temptation to interpret novel phenomena when my office is merely to invite the reader to scan these for himself in Mr. Hicks's vitally interesting presentation. If I have transgressed the proprieties of my function, the stimulating nature of his volume may suffice as an excuse.

G. L. KITTREDGE.

Contents

Illustrations

Sir Thomas Malory

Introduction

SHAKESPEARE'S genius, towering above that of all other Englishmen, has had one unfortunate effect on his native county; it has tended to focus all attention on the Swan of Avon to the almost complete neglect of other Warwickshire authors. Yet there is another name, standing high in the realm of letters, which Warwickshire folk are fully entitled to claim — that of Sir Thomas Malory, author of the *Morte d'Arthur*. Hitherto very little has been known about Malory; practically the only one to raise a corner of the thick curtain which has concealed the identity of the knight who in 1469 finished writing the immortal story of King Arthur and the Knights of the Round Table has been Professor George Lyman Kittredge, of Harvard University.[1]

Professor Kittredge made it sufficiently clear that Sir Thomas Malory came from Newbold Revel, in the parish of Monks Kirby, Warwickshire — a point which will be found emphasised by additional matter in Chapter XV of the present work. Professor Kittredge's conjectural identification of the author of the *Morte* was put on record as long ago as March, 1894, when it was announced in Johnson's *Universal Cyclopædia*. This, however, did not attract notice in England; therefore, when Mr. T. W. Williams stated in the *Athenæum* of July 11, 1896, that he had discovered among Wells Cathedral MSS a document which excluded "Thomas Malorie, *miles*," from a general pardon in 1468, he did

"Who was Sir Thomas Malory?" An article contained in vol. V of *Studies and Notes in Philology and Literature*, Boston, Mass., 1897.

not connect the Warwickshire knight with the "Malorie" to whom he had found reference, although they were really one and the same person. Later — in January, 1920 — Mr. Edward F. Cobb brought to Professor Kittredge's notice an extract from the De Banco Rolls of Henry VI, 1443, showing that Thomas Malory, *miles*, and another were charged with assault with violence at Sprotton, Northants. This affair, whatever its rights or wrongs may have been, appears to have been settled out of court.

More serious was the trouble in which Sir Thomas Malory was involved in 1451 — reference to which was made by Sir E. K. Chambers in January, 1922, in a pamphlet published by the English Association. Sir E. K. Chambers quoted the Calendar of Patent Rolls to show that some dispute had occurred between Sir Thomas and the Carthusians at Monks Kirby, which brought about the intervention of Henry VI.

The present writer's researches at the Public Record Office have brought to light the proceedings against Sir Thomas Malory, who was accused not only of offences against the Carthusians, but of leading an assault on Coombe Abbey and setting an ambush in the Abbey Woods for one of the most powerful noblemen of the day, viz., Humphrey, Duke of Buckingham, uncle (by marriage) of the King-Maker. The indictment included several other counts — to all of which Sir Thomas pleaded not guilty; but their cumulative effect on the minds of the Warwickshire Jury who tried him must have been that he was, like Sir Corsabrin, "a passing felonious knight."

Malory's early career and his subsequent long confinement in Newgate Gaol are dealt with in the present volume, which also indicates the conditions under which he wrote the *Morte*.

It is fair to assume that Professor Kittredge's interest in the subject of Malory was stimulated by the fact that America possesses the only perfect copy of the *Morte* printed by Caxton which is known to exist.[1] This was bought for £1,950 by Mrs. Norton Q. Pope at the sale of the Osterley Park Library in 1885, and taken to Brooklyn, New York. On the death of Mrs. Pope, it was purchased by Mr. Robert Hoe, of New York, and in 1911 acquired by the late Mr. J. Pierpont Morgan for $42,800. It is now in the Pierpont Morgan Library in New York City. Mr. Pierpont Morgan's son has recently made this Library a public institution (liberally endowed) under a special board of trustees. The volume is therefore at rest, and never will be sold again.

It was a recent pupil of Professor Kittredge at Harvard, Dr. J. Leslie Hotson, who in 1925 published the result of his researches at the Public Record Office concerning the death of Christopher Marlowe. Yet another American, Dr. J. Douglas Bruce (Professor of the English Language and Literature in the University of Tennessee) some years ago reëdited the metrical *Morte Arthur* for the Early English Text Society. To Englishmen, accustomed as they are to seeing the choicest MSS and books purchased by Dr. Rosenbach for shipment to the United States, it should be no small consolation to reflect that American scholars are justifying by their research work the avidity with which our literary treasures are being acquired for Transatlantic homes.

The Year Books covering the years 1455–1470 contain

[1] The only other Caxton copy, now in the Rylands Library at Manchester, has eleven leaves supplied in facsimile.

no references to Sir Thomas Malory; and to prevent the repetition of futile search, it may be well to state here that the Assize Rolls for Warwickshire and Leicestershire, the Close Rolls and the Patent Rolls for the period indicated have been searched in vain. The Coram Rege Roll for 1468, the year in which Malory was excluded from two pardons, has also been examined without result. Moreover, although it is certain that Sir Thomas's widow left a will, no trace of it is discoverable at Lichfield (where the records of the old Coventry and Lichfield diocese are kept) nor in the official archives in London.

Acknowledgment of the help given by Mr. Montague Giuseppi, Superintendent of the Legal Research Department at the Public Record Office, is made on page 19, but there are others whose assistance has been extremely valuable. Miss N. McNeill O'Farrell not only transcribed the record of the Inquisition at Nuneaton and the proceedings at Westminster, but discovered the document which bears the seal of Sir Thomas Malory's father. Mr. Philip B. Chatwin, F.S.A., F.R.I.B.A., has given the writer the benefit of his exceptional knowledge of Warwickshire archaeology, while Mr. F. J. Thacker of the Birmingham Reference Library, and Mr. W. E. Owen, the Leamington Borough Librarian, have done much to facilitate the compilation of this biography. Finally, I would acknowledge the help given by members of my family and especially by my daughter Phyllis, who not only prepared the map showing the Malory country but also compiled the index.

Chapter I

ANCESTRY AND MILITARY CAREER

Bale asserts that the author (of the *Morte d'Arthur*) was occupied with affairs of State, but practically no definite information is available respecting him outside his book. — *Dictionary of National Biography*, concerning Sir Thomas Malory.

PRIOR to the investigations of Professor G. Lyman Kittredge, the identity of Sir Thomas Malory had been a matter of speculation in many quarters. For example, Bishop Bale (1495–1563), after declaring "Thomas Mailorius" to be by race and country a Briton, recalled Leland's statement that "Mailoria" was a district within the Welsh borders, not far from the River Dee. But, to quote Professor Kittredge: "Bale's biographical statements are of the good old-fashioned sort, and convey no information. He admits that he does not even know under what king that 'Mailorius' flourished — something that he might have discovered from the closing words of the *Morte*." At one time, indeed, it was supposed that Sir Thomas was a Welsh priest — the "Sir" being regarded as the equivalent of "reverend" in translating *dominus*. Place-names are very apt to suggest wrong derivations, and a reader of the *Morte d'Arthur* who knew that in Denbighshire there was a little town named Maelor would be strongly tempted to jump to the conclusion that the author of this, the greatest of English prose romances, came from that place, especially if he were ignorant of the fact that Welshmen did not bear surnames till a good deal later than Sir Thomas Malory's time — Henry VII's reign, to be precise.[1]

The writer of the *Morte*, it is now clear, belonged to a family whose ancestor [2] came over with the Conqueror, and established himself at Kirkby Malory, in Leicestershire. Sir Stephen Malory — great grandfather of Sir Thomas — acquired a footing in Warwickshire (*temp.* Edward III) by marrying Margaret Revell, heiress to the Fenny Newbold estates. The status of the family is shown by the fact that it furnished sheriffs of Warwickshire and Leicestershire in 15 Richard II, 4 Henry V, and 3 Henry VI.[3] Sir Thomas's own father, John Malory, *armiger*, was M.P. for Warwickshire in 1413, 1419, 1423, and 1427. An even more onerous duty was his in 1424, when he was appointed Escheator for Warwickshire and Leicestershire, and so became responsible to the Crown for estates the owners of which had died intestate. He married Philippa Chetwynd, of Grendon, in the County of Warwick — a marriage which, incidentally, seems to have made him a party, with Sir John Cockayne, Kt. and John Chetwynd, to the lawsuits which were carried on for years concerning land at Meriden (then known as Alspath). A nephew of Philippa Malory was "a person not a little eminent in his time" — we refer to Sir Philip Chetwynd, the fifth of that name. Born about 1400, he, like his cousin Thomas, was taken into the Earl of Warwick's service and in 1428 placed about the person of the little king, Henry VI.

---

[1] The object was to enable the authorities to keep better supervision of "undesirables."

[2] "Mallory" in Holinshed's *Roll of Battel Abbey.* "Malory" in Stow's *Chronicles.*

[3] Fuller's *Worthies.* It should be noted that the two counties were linked under one sheriff until 9 Eliz.

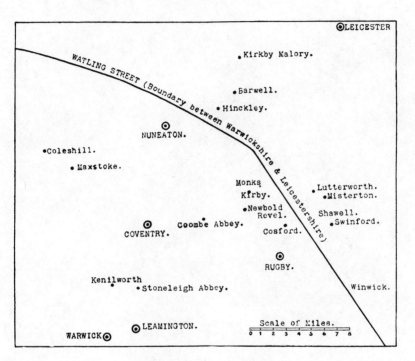

THE MALORY COUNTRY.

Subsequently Sir Philip was appointed Governor of Bayonne, — "where the wine of Beaume is," comments Malory appreciatively in the *Morte*, — and in the self-same year (1442) Sir Thomas [1] was one of the witnesses to a settlement of the Chetwynd estates in Warwickshire and Staffordshire on Sir Philip and Joan his wife.

Dugdale's *Antiquities of Warwickshire* contains several reproductions of what is described as the Malory coat-of-arms, together with the cognizance of the Revells; but Sir Thomas Malory's father, at all events, did not use the coat-of-arms assigned by Dugdale to his family, viz.: *Or, 3 Lyons Passant, Gardant Sa.*[2] This is proved by the wax seal attached to a deed of 12 Henry VI preserved at the Public Record Office.[3] By this document, dated shortly before his death, John Malory granted an annual rent of 12d. and three capons in respect of land at Wibtoft. The wax seal is identical with the coat-of-arms depicted in the pages of Papworth [4] as belonging to the Malory family, viz.,

Erm. a chev. between three 3-foils slipped arg. a bordurè eng. sa.

It is interesting to compare this with the armorial bearings depicted on the cloak worn by Philippa, mother of Sir Thomas Malory, which are distinctly "Revell" in appearance (see Frontispiece). The dresses of ladies of that period were decorated with the arms of their families, so that when — as we read in the *Morte* — a knight wore a lady's sleeve in his helmet, it would have

---

[1] The Chetwynd Cartulary — which shows also that Malory had been knighted by this time.

[2] Fuller, in his *Worthies*, assigns this badge to the Leicestershire branch of the Malorys.

[3] Court of Wards (Deeds and Evidences), Box 1.

[4] J. W. Papworth, *Ordinary of British Armorals.*

been quickly identified, as no doubt it was intended to be.

As a member of the Retinue of Richard Beauchamp, Earl of Warwick, the author of the *Morte* saw military service in France at the period when Joan of Arc's inspiring presence had turned the tide against the English. Seeing that Richard Beauchamp furnished the special guard posted in Rouen market-place when Joan was burnt in 1431, it is highly probable that Malory was present on that occasion. One whom he was to face twenty years later in very different circumstances was also present — Humphrey, Earl of Stafford (afterwards Duke of Buckingham). As Constable of France for Henry VI, the latter had had more than one interview with Joan in her prison at Rouen. His ideas of knightly courtesy are illustrated by the following incidents. The Pucelle having declared that "Were there one hundred thousand *godons* more than at present, they would not conquer the kingdom," the Earl of Stafford (as he then was) unsheathed his sword, so that the Earl of Warwick had to restrain his hand. That the English Constable of France would have raised his sword against a woman in chains would be incredible did we not know that about this time the Earl of Stafford, hearing someone speak well of Joan, straightway wished to transfix him.[1]

Dugdale mentions, as an important item of Malory's war record, that he served in the garrison "at the siege of Caleys in King Henry V's time, being of the retinue of Richard Beauchamp, Earl of Warwick." As a matter of fact, however, there was no siege of Calais in this reign, although, early in 1414, when the Earl was appointed Deputy of the fortress, a French attack was

[1] Anatole France.

anticipated. Dugdale gives as his authority in this instance "Rot(ulus) in bibl. Hatton." Search for this Roll at the Bodleian Library and the British Museum has proved fruitless, and we are forced to conclude that it was among the valuable MSS, etc., destroyed in the great fire at the Birmingham Public Library in 1879. The same Roll, however, is cited by Dugdale as his authority for statements concerning other members of Richard Beauchamp's retinue, and it is by examining these references that we are able approximately to establish the date at which Malory served at Calais. To begin with, Dugdale is by no means always consistent on the point of there having been a *siege* of Calais in the reign of Henry V. For example, of Sir Ralph Bracebridge of Kingsbury he says that he was retained to serve the Earl "for the strengthening of Calais." Again, of Sir William de Bishopton we are told that he was retained by the Earl of Warwick "for the fortifying of Calais." On the other hand, Sir Ralph Arden of Curdworth and John de L'Isle of Moxhull are stated to have been two of the Earl's esquires "at the siege of Calais"; and if the categorical statement made regarding Sir William Mountford of Coleshill could really be accepted literally, it would follow that Malory was present at the brief siege of Calais in 1406. This, however, is incredible, for he must have been a mere lad at the time; and, moreover, Richard Beauchamp had not as yet been appointed Captain of Calais. We know that one member of the retinue, Sir Ralph Arden, died in 1421; consequently it must have been during a captaincy prior to that date that Malory served under the Earl at Calais. We know that the Earl was first appointed Captain of Calais on February 3, 1414; but a few days earlier he was ordered, in that capacity, to proclaim a truce. On October 20, 1414, he was commissioned to go to the Council of Constance, and this caused an interruption in his captaincy. When he resumed the office, he did so under an indenture of June 19, 1415, by which he agreed "to serve the King as Captain of Calais until February 3, 1416. And to have with him in the time of Truce or Peace, for the safeguard thereof, Thirty Men at Arms, himself and three Knights accounted as part of that number; Thirty Archers on Horsback, Two Hundred Foot Soldiers, and Two hundred Archers, all of his own retinue. . . . And in time of War, he to have One hundred and forty Men on Horsbak," etc.[1] We may conclude, therefore, that the Roll which Dugdale cited as his authority bore date 1414 or 1415.

The point is important in another respect, for it helps us to estimate Malory's age. We read in the *Morte* that when Sir Bors desired to take his fifteen-year-old son with him on a knightly expedition, King Arthur objected. "Ye may well take him with you, but he is over tender of age." It is true that Malory makes Elaine say: "My lord Sir Launcelot, at this same feast of Pentecost shall your son and mine, Galahad, be made knight, for he is fully now fifteen winter old." This is one of the numerous passages which Malory has inserted "on his own," so to speak. But against this we must place Chaucer's description of

A young squier
A lover and a lusty bacheler;
· · · · · · · ·
Of twenty yer of age he was I gesse.

[1] Dugdale's *Baronage*, i, 244.

The young man who in 1415 was accompanied by a lance and two archers when he joined the Earl of Warwick's retinue must have been something like 21 years of age. Hence when Sir Thomas Malory died in March, 1471, he must have been somewhere about 77 years old. If it be objected that this is scarcely credible, the reply must be that Malory was not the only septuagenarian of his day and county. John Rous, the Warwick antiquary, who was a lad when Richard Beauchamp founded the chantry at Guy's Cliffe in 1423, died in 1491 at the reputed age of 81. John Hardyng, a strictly contemporary writer, who was present at the battle of Agincourt, died somewhere about 1465 "at a great old age." [1]

As a member of the Retinue of Richard Beauchamp, the "Father of Courtesie," Sir Thomas Malory had full opportunity of studying one whom the world of chivalry, both in Europe and in the Holy Land, regarded as its *beau idéal*.

Whether or no Sir Thomas Malory, as a page, accompanied Richard Beauchamp on his world tour, it is certain that he benefited by the knowledge his lord had gained by travel. "The details (given in the *Morte*) of King Arthur's march to Rome are so accurate that I think that Malory may have had actual knowledge of the road," wrote the late Sir Edward Strachey, 3rd Baronet, in his preface to the very able edition published by him in 1868. Dr. Oskar Sommer, indeed, sug-

[1] Malory, when he died, must have been a mere lad compared with Johan Grauntpe, of Coventry, who, according to *Early Chancery Proceedings*, was 140 when he made complaint to the Chancellor of England that he and Agnes his wife had been unjustly deprived of a close called "Dudmounesfeld," worth 40s. a year. Certain feoffees, he alleged, would not let him enter therein because he is an old man aged 140, blind, decrepit, sick and bedridden, poor and feeble, ("a cause qil est veill homme dage de $\overset{xx}{vij}$ anz aveogls decrepit malade en sounz lite continuelment gisaunt povre et feble").

gests that geographical knowledge is not Malory's strong point, this criticism being based on the mention of "Sandwich" as the place where Arthur's armies gather and set out to sea. "Considering that Arthur planned to, and really did, cross over to Normandy," adds Dr. Sommer, "it is more natural that Southampton should be the port chosen than Sandwich in Kent." Against this we have the actual record of troops having embarked at Sandwich in Henry V's reign.[1]

In many lands Richard Beauchamp displayed his prowess, so that the Emperor Sigismund, when visiting Henry V, was heard to declare "That no Christian Prince hath such another Knight for Wisdom, Nurture and Manhood, that if all Courtesie were lost, yet it might be found again in him." And so, ever after, by the Emperor's authority, he was called "the Fadre of Curteisy." It is this nobleman whom Mr. George Bernard Shaw has seen fit, in "St. Joan," to represent as the cynic of his period! In the absence of information as to the precise date of Sir Thomas Malory's birth, it is impossible to say whether he accompanied the Earl in his *Wanderjähre*, which extended from 1408 to 1410; but we know that the struggle with France, which entered on a more violent phase when Henry V ascended the throne, did not put a stop to those deeds of knight-errantry which figure so prominently in the pages of the *Morte*. When Richard Beauchamp was first appointed Captain of Calais (in 1411) a French attack was anticipated, but when the danger passed, the Earl "resolved to put in practice some new point of chivalry." He therefore caused three shields to be made, and in each of them a lady painted, whose cause was to be championed respec-

[1] Exchequer Accounts, Q.R., 50/1, 9 Hen. V.

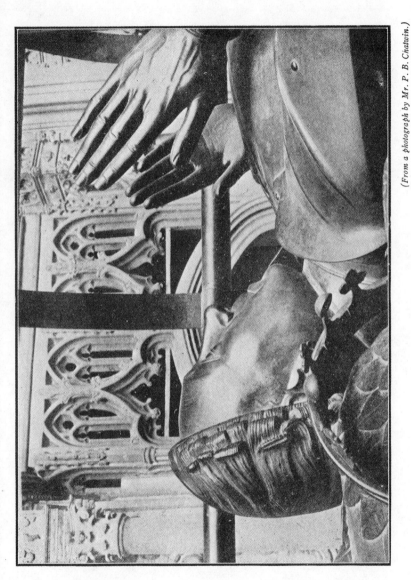

THE TOMB OF RICHARD BEAUCHAMP, EARL OF WARWICK, MALORY'S FEUDAL CHIEF.

tively by the Green Knight, the Chivalier Vert, and the Chivalier Attendant. In each of these guises the Earl was victorious, in so much that the Frenchmen alleged that he had bound himself to his saddle. Alighting in the presence of the assembly, he proved the baselessness of the accusation, and having feasted all the people and given handsome mementoes to his three opponents, he returned to Calais with great honour.[1]

Association with such a dashing and altogether attractive personality must have helped to colour Malory's whole outlook, of which we have striking evidence in the *Morte*. According to Dugdale, Malory served in the French Wars with one lance and two archers, receiving for his lance and one archer £20 per annum and their diet, and for the other archer 10 marks without diet. Exactly how to express these sums in terms of present-day currency is a difficult problem. As a writer on the history of Exchange has said: "Even now there are country districts in England where money will go half as far again as it would do in some of our great towns. But in old times the difference was infinitely greater, so that there is no possibility of gauging the difference between the old and the present values of money by any equational system." Dugdale, after recording that Richard Beauchamp left estate valued at 8306 marks 11s. 11d., attempts in his own way to arrive at the value of the sum. "At the time," he writes, "barley was sold for 4s. 2d. per quarter, oats at 2s. 1d., capons at 3d. apiece, and hens at 1d."

As the Earl of Warwick was not present at the battle of Agincourt, in October, 1415, it is to be inferred that Malory also was not there; but that Sir Thomas saw

[1] Dugdale's *Antiquities of Warwickshire*.

much military service in France is clear from the fact
that his name is absent from the lists of M.P.s and Sheriffs for Warwickshire while the war lasted, and that immediately the long struggle was over he represented his
county in Parliament. As a member of the retinue of
Richard Beauchamp he would accompany the Earl in
1436 to the relief of Calais, when the fortress was be-
sieged by the Burgundians. It is worthy of note that
the chief command of the relieving force was entrusted
to Humphrey, Duke of Gloucester, in his day the chief
patron of letters in this country, and the real founder of
the Bodleian Library. Richard Beauchamp's regard for
learning is also on record; he presented a copy of the
Decameron to Duke Humphrey, and it was at his instance that Lydgate, the poet, wrote his metrical account of the English claims to the French throne. Lydgate thus attested the fact:

> I moved was shortly in sentiment
> By precept first and commaundement
> Of the nobly prince and manly man,
> Which is so knyghtly and so moche can,
> My lord of Warrewyk, so prudent and wise.

Thus the circumstances of Malory's military service
were rather favourable than otherwise to the growth in
him of an interest in literature. The perpetual hand-to-
hand combats met with in the *Morte* can also be explained by Malory's experience in the French Wars. A
particular instance in point may be cited. In 1438 —
within twelve months after Paris had been recaptured
from the English — a near relative of the Earl of Warwick took advantage of a pause in hostilities to visit the
French capital and "maintain a duel on horseback
within the street called St. Antoine [adjacent to the

Bastille] against one Peter de Masse, a Frenchman, in the presence of Charles VII." The English champion was Sir John de Astley, of Patshull,[1] "who pierced the said Peter through the head and had his helmet to present unto his lady." This incident happened, not, as might be supposed, while the opposing armies were in winter-quarters, but in the month of August. Could a more telling example be quoted of the fifteenth-century passion for duelling, jousts, tournaments, which the *Morte* associates with a much earlier period? It should be added that so famous for valour did Sir John de Astley grow that early in the reign of Edward IV he was elected a Knight of the Garter. As has been well said, "the 14th and 15th centuries saw the Court of Chivalry at its best and strongest. The insight given by the Hundred Years War into the privileged position of the aristocracy in France doubtless contributed to a demand on the part of the quality in England for the maintenance of a Court that dealt with questions in which points of honour were concerned; with mere personal affronts."

[1] Dugdale's *Antiquities*. Sir John de Astley's sister Joan married Thomas Appelby. It seems probable that the latter was related to John Appelby, Sir Thomas Malory's aider and abetter in the outbreak of 1451.

Chapter II

PARLIAMENTARY SERVICE

W E NEXT catch sight of Sir Thomas Malory in
1445, when, the Hundred Years War having
come to an inglorious end, he was free to return to Newbold Revel. There, "being a knight, he served for this
shire in the Parliament then held at Westminster." [1]
It is highly interesting to observe the two names associated with his in the Fine Roll of 23 Henry VI. One is
that of Humphrey, Duke of Buckingham, the other is
that of Sir William Mountford, of Coleshill. Six years
later we shall see the latter arresting Malory and the
Duke presiding at his trial.

The Parliament of 1445 in which Sir Thomas sat had
some most important business to transact. We learn
from Hansard that writs were issued on January 13 for
the Parliament to meet at Westminster on February 25.
In the presence of the King, sitting in person in his chair
of state, and of the Lords and Commons, John Stafford,
late Bishop of Bath and Wells, but now Archbishop and
Chancellor of England, declared the cause of calling this
Parliament, namely, to ratify the marriage treaty ar-
ranged between the King and Margaret, daughter of the
King of Sicily. Parliament was then prorogued to April
19, when the Chancellor made protestation "that the
peace which the King had made with the French king,
or rather was about to make, was merely of his own mo-

[1] Dugdale's *Antiquities*.

tion and will and that he was not instigated thereto by himself or any of the lords whatsoever." Which protest was enrolled. Thereupon it was decided that the statute of Henry V "importing that no peace should be made with the French King that now is, and was then called Dauphin of France, without the assent of the three Estates of both realms should be utterly repealed and revoked, and that no person whatsoever should be impeached at any time to come for giving counsel to bring about this peace with France." Thus was indemnified the Earl of Suffolk, who had promoted the treaty. It availed little to save him five years later, when he was murdered on the way to banishment.

Another Act concerned the "wages" of Members of Parliament — the manner of their election — the remedy where one is chosen and another returned. Parliament also confirmed the King's letters patent for the erection and endowment of Eton College and King's College, Cambridge. (The endowment, by the way, was derived from the revenues of a large number of "alien" monasteries which had recently been dissolved.)

Sir Thomas Malory's name, although it appears in the Fine Roll already referred to, is not in the printed list compiled from the Writs of Summons to Parliament, and the fact that in the following year the name of Edmund Mountford, *armiger*, is so included "gives one furiously to think." For Sir Edmund (as he afterwards became) was a younger son, by a second marriage, of that Sir William Mountford who arrested Malory in 1451 (see page 30), and in view of what is known about him and the Duke of Buckingham, it appears extremely probable that he supplanted Malory in the Parliamentary representation of Warwickshire, just as he supplanted his brother, Sir Baldwin, in regard to the manor of Coleshill. Sir Edmund, it is to be noted, had been appointed an esquire to Henry VI in 1444, and was, "indeed, much in favour with that unfortunate prince."[1] All the weight of the Duke of Buckingham's influence would naturally be given to Edmund in view of the understanding that had been arrived at between them as to the possession of Coleshill. The "management of elections" had at this period become a scandal, although it was an obvious result of the restriction of the franchise which had just taken place. The complaint of the Kentish-men in Cade's revolt alleges that "the people of the shire are not allowed to have their free election in the choosing of knights for the shire, but letters have been sent from divers estates to the great rulers of all the county, the which enforceth their tenants and other people by force to choose other persons than the common will is."[2]

[1] Dugdale, *Antiquities.*
[2] J. R. Green, *History of the English People.*

Chapter III

A "RIGHT WILD" ENGLAND

FROM Sir Thomas Malory, Knight of the Shire representing his county in Parliament, to Sir Thomas Malory arraigned for armed assaults on monasteries in Warwickshire is a startling change. Without some knowledge of the period in question, the change would appear too violent to be credited. "The lawlessness of the country at this time," says Professor Ransome, "was such as had not been tolerated in England for many centuries." The loss of Normandy and the heavy load of taxation which had to be borne as a result of the struggle with France would in any case have made the task of government difficult; but matters were worsened by other evils, among which must be reckoned the removal of bishops from their dioceses in order to perform State duties in London. Thus, the Bishop of Coventry and Lichfield had been called from his proper sphere in order to act as chancellor to Queen Margaret of Anjou. It was the neglect of the bishops and clergy to do their several duties that led to Jack Cade's insurrection in 1450, wrote Dr. Gascoigne, an anti-Lollard. As the civil servants of the period, they no doubt could have retorted that they were fulfilling duties which no one else was then qualified to perform. In any case, the Bishop must have had an unenviable task in acting as chancellor to "England's dear-bought queen." So preoccupied was he with his duties at Court that his episcopal register contains not a single reference to the stormy days of July, 1451, in his diocese.

The Patent Rolls record innumerable instances of the state of confusion and uneasiness that prevailed. In March of this same year (1451) the Bishop of Bath and Wells had been given permission to enclose the ecclesiastical buildings at Wells with a stone wall "and crenellate the same and make towers there for the greater security of the Bishop and Canons." One of the Pastons' correspondents warned his master that "the world is right wild." He was thinking more particularly of Norfolk. Documents now brought to light at the Public Record Office and set forth in Chapter VI prove that Warwickshire was also "wild." Coventry was one of the hot-beds of a militant Lollardy which in 1431 had made demonstration against the hierarchy. Their leader, "Jack Sharpe of Wygmoreland," had distributed pamphlets which took the form of a petition to the King and Lords in Parliament showing the waste which ensued from the possession of temporalities by bishops, abbots, and priors of the Church, and praying for their resumption by the Crown.[1] At that date, however, the central government was strong, with the result that no mercy was shown, all persons implicated being treated as guilty of high treason.

It is important to remember that, living at Newbold Revel, his principal manor, Sir Thomas Malory would be only six miles from Lutterworth, the fountain-head of Lollardy. Wycliffe himself, early in 1382, had urged the gradual confiscation of all clerical property by special taxation.[2] The grievance of paying tithe to a dis-

---

[1] K. H. Vickers, *Humphrey Duke of Gloucester.*
[2] Dr. James Gairdner.

tant religious house had, in the previous year, driven
men near Melton Mowbray to join Wat Tyler's rebellion, under the leadership of a curate from a neighbour-
ing village.¹ Similar cases occurred elsewhere. In bad
times, such as England experienced immediately after
the Hundred Years War, the strict demand for tithe
pressed hard on the poor, and the movement for refusal
of such dues was at this period a marked thing.²

The demand for payment of heriots when a monastic
tenant died was also a grievance at this time, as Warwickshire history proves. A great riot took place at
Shipston-on-Stour in the sixth year of Henry VI, with
reference to heriots, and the question was ultimately
referred to the Abbot of Winchcombe, who determined
that the prior and convent of Worcester had from early
times received at the death of every tenant the best
animal, while the parson of Tredington received the
second best.

"It was really not the theological doctrines half so
much as the external polity of the Church that Wycliffe
called in question," says Dr. Gairdner. But the Act of
Parliament passed against Lollardy twenty-two years
after Wycliffe's death shows the apprehension that the
movement had excited by this time in the breasts of the
ruling classes. "If the designs of these persons were not
resisted," it was declared, "they would in time succeed
in depriving the temporal lords likewise of their possessions, which they would treat as common property and
thus raise commotions which would be the complete
destruction of the Kingdom." How very modern it
sounds! The attitude of the House of Lancaster toward
Lollardy had not been made more friendly by what hap-

¹ André Reville.   ² G. M. Trevelyan.

pened at the end of 1417 — only two years after Agincourt. While Henry V was spending his Christmas at
Kenilworth, it is recorded, a squire of Sir John Oldcastle's laid an ambush for him.[1]

That discontent with the monastic system was not
confined to Lollards, however, is clear. Richard Fox,
Bishop of Winchester, was persuaded by Bishop Old-
ham of Exeter to found Corpus Christi College, Oxford,
rather than "provide livelodes for a companie of buss-
ing monks."[2] Even when the bishops insisted on a
settled sum from impropriated livings being put on one
side for the parish priest, the regular clergy (the monasteries) tried to cut this down as much as possible.[3]
"The practice of impropriation has been regarded by
most writers as a manifest abuse, and there is no call to
attempt to defend it."[4] On the other hand, it is urged
that "the churches and vicarages of places impropriated
were the special care of the religious. An examination
of these churches frequently reveals the fact that religious bodies did not hesitate to spend large sums of
money upon the rebuilding and adornment of structures
which belonged to them in this way."[5]

[1] Ramsay's *Lancaster and York*, i, 254.
[2] A. Abram, *English Life and Manners in the Later Middle Ages*.
[3] H. S. Bennett, *The Pastons and their England*.
[4] Cardinal Gasquet, *English Monastic Life*.
[5] *Ibid*.

Chapter IV

THE QUEST

SIR E. K. CHAMBERS, after noting Professor Kittredge's discovery of Sir Thomas Malory's identity,
had observed that in July, 1451, the knight of Newbold
Revel was ordered to find sureties for good behaviour
towards the Priory of Axholme, Lincs., a Carthusian
monastery to which the revenues of Monks Kirby had
been granted. Further, that he was arrested in March,
1453, presumably because of some renewal of the dispute.[1] A search of the Warwickshire Assize Rolls for the
period was suggested to the present writer as a likely
method of gaining further information; but although a
good deal of county interest was gleaned in the course
of the search, nothing relating to Malory himself was
encountered. There was, of course, always a doubt
whether the trial — if any — was held in Warwickshire
or in London. A survey of the Indictments from Middlesex was a task to baulk the most enthusiastic enquirer;
but there remained one other section which might con-
ceivably yield fruit. This was calendered as "Divers
Counties." A few words of encouragement from Mr.
Montague S. Giuseppi, I.S.O., Superintendent of the
Legal Research Department, sped the writer to his task,
and after a prolonged turning over of parchment strips
— some long, some short, and all more or less faded —
and noting how in the fifteenth century the counties of

[1] Patent Rolls.

"Myddx." and Essex appeared to be responsible for most of the crime of England, the welcome words "In Com. Warr." attracted attention. Warwickshire, then, was represented among the "Divers Counties" in this *dossier*. Closer examination of the parchment showed that it concerned some stabbing affray in the streets of Warwick; "glaives" were the weapons used.

Stimulated to a further search, the writer continued to turn over the strips of parchment, and after more time had been devoted to the task the words "In Com. Warr." once again jumped to the eye.

The document, of course, was in Latin, and a portion of the right-hand edge of it had been somewhat damaged; but, half-way down, the eye was caught and held by two words — "Thomas Malory" — written with almost copperplate clearness. The hunt was over, the quarry secured! One more proof had been found that the Public Record Office is a veritable treasure-house for those desiring to throw light on the mysteries of the past.

The Record of the Inquisition held regarding Sir Thomas Mallory's alleged misdeeds had been found.[1] But it was very surprising to read that it was held at Nuneaton, seeing that Coventry — a more important centre — was nearer the places concerned, and was in fact on the point of becoming an Assize town — by Royal Charter dated Nov. 26, 1451. Moreover, St. Mary's Hall in that city — which had been built a few years previously — would have been a most commodious place in which to hold the enquiry.

The probable explanation is that Coventry at this period was "a special nest of heresy," and therefore un-

[1] See Appendix.

suitable as the venue of a trial of persons charged with attacks on monastic houses.

Coventry's unsuitability for the purpose, indeed, was beyond question, as was proved by an incident which happened there a few years earlier. In 1423 the Lollard views of John Grace, an enthusiastic anchorite friar, "met with great favour from lower classes, and when the (Benedictine) Prior of Coventry and the Grey Friars opposed him, alleging that his preacher's licence had been withdrawn, they were nearly killed by the mob." [1]

On the other hand, Nuneaton, in the fifteenth century, comprised little besides "a goodly monasterie" belonging to Benedictine nuns — founded in connection with the parent house at Fontevrault in Normandy. Their Chapter House suggests itself as the place in which the Inquisition was held, and that it was big enough for the purpose is clear from the fact that at one time the nunnery had ninety inmates, although in 1450 there were only half that number. But quite possibly the Inquisition was held in the Abbey Church, or in the Parish Church of St. Nicholas. "Mediæval churches were put to strange uses. They served sometimes as a market place, sometimes as a granary, sometimes as a stage." [2]

[1] *Victoria County History of Warwickshire.*

[2] Eileen Power, *Mediæval Nunneries.* Some three months after the holding of the Inquisition, the Prioress, Maud Evryngham (daughter of Sir Henry Evryngham?), made complaint that the convent was impoverished, and was granted relief from the exactions of the King's purveyors. (Patent Roll.)

Chapter V

A POWERFUL ANTAGONIST

THE Inquisition was held on Monday, August 23, 1451, and was presided over by Humphrey, Duke of Buckingham, whom Malory would remember meeting in the old days at Rouen when Joan of Arc suffered martyrdom.[1] The Duke had just finished punishing Jack Cade's followers at Rochester, and he was now to act as judge upon an indictment in which he was personally concerned. Just as his grandfather had punished those concerned in Wat Tyler's rebellion, so Duke Humphrey, with relentless vigour, had quelled a Lollard rising in 1431 in the neighbourhood of Kenilworth and Coventry.[2] Ten years later he had been a member of the special Commission which tried Eleanor Cobham on a charge of witchcraft. Seeing that one of the charges to be preferred against Sir Thomas Malory was that of lying in ambush to attack the Duke, the latter — according to twentieth-century notions of legal procedure — would have done well to decline sitting on the Bench on this occasion. But the Duke was not one to be fastidious in a matter of this sort.

Parliament in Richard II's reign had indeed enacted that great lords were not to assert their powers by seating themselves with the King's Judges; but public opin-

[1] Grandson of Thomas of Woodstock, and great-grandson of Edward III, the Duke had just been appointed Captain of Calais and Warden of the Cinque Ports.
[2] Privy Council Ordinances.

ion no more prevented the Duke of Buckingham from acting as judge in his own cause than it deterred "Mr Justice Shallow" more than a century later from adjudicating in a certain case of deer-stealing in his domain. Less than a hundred years ago, indeed, — in 1830, — it was possible at Wiltshire Quarter Sessions for the presiding magistrate to sentence to fourteen years' transportation a poor fellow charged with stealing a plank ten feet long, the property of the aforesaid magnate. The Duke of Buckingham might, at all events, have excused his action by saying that the Inquisition at Nuneaton was in reality a sort of Grand Jury proceeding, and that the question of punishment was left to the King's Bench at Westminster.

Duke Humphrey, who had married into the great Neville family, — great in more senses than one, for Ralph, Earl of Westmorland, had 23 children, of whom all but one attained full age, — counted possessions in seven and twenty counties. Some nineteen years before the date of which we are speaking he had acquired, by exchange with the Clintons, the castle of Maxsoke, in Warwickshire. For this place he had "a very great liking," and in view of the probability that Sir Thomas Malory was imprisoned there for a time before his trial at Nuneaton, — after his escape from the Sheriff's custody at Coleshill, — Dugdale's reference to the castle will be read with interest. "No sooner did he [the Duke] obtain it, but that he plated the Gates all over with Iron, and adorn'd them with his own Coat, impaled with Neville (his Wife being the Daughter to Ralphe Neville, Earl of Westmorland) and supported by two Antelopes, in Respect that Anne, his Mother, was one of the Daughters and Co-heirs unto Thomas of Woodstoke, Duke of

Gloucester. And in further Memorie that these Gates were so strengthened and beautified, he caused the burning Nave and Knot (the antient Badges of his Ancestors) to be imbossed in the Iron-Work thwarting the Midst thereof, as are yet to be seen. This great Earl being created Duke of Buckingham (in 1445), constituted William Draicote his Constable of this Castle; for executing which Office he had the Fee of five Marks per annum."

We have said that Humphrey, Duke of Buckingham, was not one to be fastidious. An episode given in Dugdale's *Antiquities of Warwickshire* will serve to prove this, and also, it may be, to explain why Sir Thomas Malory should have lain in ambush for the Duke. A dispute over possession of the manor of Coleshill lay at the root of the matter. Since 1354 the Mountford family had been lords of Coleshill, and Sir William Mountford had served with Malory in the retinue of Richard Beauchamp, and been "Chief of the Councell unto the same Earl and Executor unto the Ladie Isabell his Countess." At the time the trouble with Sir Thomas Malory came to a head, Sir William was serving his third term of office as Sheriff of Warwickshire and Leicestershire, and when ordered to arrest the knight of Newbold Revel, his former comrade-in-arms, he decided to keep him in custody at Coleshill rather than place him in gaol at the recognised prison in Warwick or Kenilworth.[1]

High-handed action on the part of Sir William Mountford at a somewhat later date is indicated by *Early Chancery Proceedings*. Margerie Mariot, of Coventry, complains that her son William was arrested by the city

---

[1] Royal Commissions to hold General Gaol-deliveries at Warwick and Kenilworth are recorded at this period.

Humphery Duke of Buckingham.

THE DUKE WHO PRESIDED AT MALORY'S TRIAL
AT NUNEATON.

officers because he intervened to protect his father from assault by John Couper, and was kept in prison "half a yere and more" by the Sheriff without any suit being brought against him. Those who would have gone bail for him were afraid to do so — "ther durste noe man for feir and drede of the seid Sir William him mainprise ne take to baill. . . . And the seid Sir William proposeth to holde him unto the tyme that he by duresse and longe emprisonment myght compelle the seid William Fader [*i. e.*, the father of the imprisoned man] to agree and satisfie the seid John Couper atte his own wille."

Coleshill Old Hall no longer exists, — it was demolished in 1810, — but there are still clear traces of the moat, which in the fifteenth century must have been both deep and wide. In winter-time it still fills with water from the river Cole flowing past the Mountford stronghold. Here it was that in 1575 Lettice, Countess of Essex, received clandestine visits from Robert Dudley, Earl of Leicester, a footbridge being specially constructed over the moat and pool at the back of the house leading into the park, to enable him to evade observation.

By the law of primogeniture, Sir William Mountford's son, Sir Baldwin (at this date 38 years of age), was heir to the manor of Coleshill; but, unhappily for him, he had a Breton step-mother, who conspired to gain the birthright for her own son, Edmund. Sir William, "being wrought upon by the Importunitie of Joane, his second wife, did endeavour the Disherison of his Children by the first; for the better bearing out whereof he enfeoft Humphrey, Duke of Buckingham (a potent Man in that Age) to the Use of the same Joane, and of Edmund, his son by her. Which Edmund, to make the said

Duke the more firm to his Interest, settled the Reversion, in Case he should have no Issue, upon him, and Humphrey, Earl Stafford, his son: So that when Sir Baldwin made his claim thereunto, the Duke, through his Greatness, so terrified him with Threats, that he forced him solemnly to disclaim the former Intail." Both Sir Thomas Malory and his lieutenant John Appelby would be well acquainted with the Mountford family, — Sir William Mountford's father had served with an Appelby in John of Gaunt's Spanish expedition, — and it is possible that, in the spirit of knight-errantry, Sir Thomas took the lead in an endeavour to prevent what he regarded as a gross injustice.[1] It was in such circumstances, therefore, that Malory faced his accusers at Nuneaton on the Monday preceding St. Bartholomew's Day, 1451.

[1] For further reference to Sir Baldwin Mountford, see p. 83.

Chapter VI

THE INQUISITION AT NUNEATON

SEATED on the Bench at Nuneaton with the Duke were Sir William Birmyngham (Sheriff-designate of the County) and two other Keepers of the Peace, Thomas Bate, Esq., of Arley, and Thomas Greswold, Esq., of Solihull. Greswold, it is important to note, was King's Sergeant as well as Coroner for the county of Warwick — an office which in the 15th century was somewhat equivalent to that of Public Prosecutor. For example, he was required by statute to go ". . . where houses are broken," and he was responsible for the attachment of criminals in cases of violence. Not long before this he had been acting in a judicial capacity against the Kentish rebels. Thomas Bate, the other member of the Commission, was at this time Escheator for Warwickshire. It will be seen, therefore, that the Commissioners were all men of exceptional prominence in the county — a proof of the importance which attached to the occasion.

Fifteen jurors, drawn from North Warwickshire, were empanelled and sworn, and after hearing the evidence they declared on oath:

(1) That Sir Thomas Malory, with his aider and abettor, John Appelby, gentleman, of Newbold Revel, had been arrested on Sunday, July 25, 1451, in pursuance of a royal warrant issued to the Duke of Bucking-

ham and Richard Neville, Earl of Warwick,[1] and at Coventry had been committed to the Sheriff's custody to await his trial before the King and Council on certain charges already preferred against him.[2]

(2) That on the Tuesday next ensuing, when in the custody of the Sheriff [Sir William Mountford] at Coleshill, the said Thomas broke out of prison during the night and swam across the moat there, thus evading the custody of the Sheriff. [As mediæval moats were tremendously deep and wide, and full of sewage, this was indeed an achievement.]

(3) That the said Thomas Malory and John Appelby, with half-a-score other yeomen, husbandmen, and grooms [mentioned by name], assembled on the following day "with many other malefactors and breakers of the King's peace in the manner of an insurrection," and unanimously rising, broke by night into the Abbey of Blessed Mary of Coombe — a Cistercian monastery midway between Newbold Revel and Coventry — and with great baulks of wood broke and entered divers gates and doors of the said monastery. Further, that they broke open two of the Abbot's chests and feloniously took and carried away a bag containing £21, another containing £25 gold and silver marks, and many other jewels and ornaments of the church of the said monastery, to the value of £40.

(4) That Thomas Malory, Knight, and 26 other [unknown] malefactors and breakers of the King's Peace, armed and arrayed in warlike manner, on January 4,

---

[1] The "King-Maker"; son-in-law of Malory's old chief in the French Wars.

[2] In respect of offences at Monks Kirby complained of by the Prior of the Carthusians.

FACSIMILE OF A PORTION OF THE MS. RECORDING THE INQUISITION AT NUNEATON.

1450, lay in ambush in Coombe Abbey Woods to kill and murder Humphrey, Duke of Buckingham.

(5) That Thomas Malory, Knight, Richard Malory of Radclyff near Leicester, Esq., John Appelby, and some dozen others [all named], assembled in warlike manner with many other malefactors and breakers of the King's peace to the number of 100, on Thursday, July 29, 1451, and riotously broke 18 doors of Coombe Abbey, and insulted the Abbot,[1] his monks and servants. Further, that they broke open three iron chests, corded and sealed, and feloniously stole £40 4s. 4d. found in divers bags, three gold rings set with precious stones, two silver signets, a pair of psalters, two silver zones, three pairs of beads [of coral, "laumber," and "jete"], two bows and three sheaves of arrows, the goods and chattels of the aforesaid Abbot.

(6) That Thomas Malory, Knight, and John Appelby took 20s. extortionately by threats and oppression from John Mylner at Monks Kirby on August 31, 1450; and in the same manner 100s. from Margaret Kyng and William Hales on May 31, 1450, also at Monks Kirby.

(7) That Thomas Malory, Knight, on the Saturday before Pentecost, 1450, broke into the house of Hugh Smyth at Monks Kirby and feloniously raped Joan, the wife of the said Hugh.

(8) That Thomas Malory, knight, on Thursday, August 1, 1450, feloniously raped Joan, the wife of Hugh Smyth, at Coventry, and carried away to Barwell, co. Leicester, goods and chattels of the said Hugh, to the value of £40.

---

[1] Abbot Richard must have fully expected the same fate that befel his predecessor, Abbot Geoffrey, in 1345, viz., a violent death.

On another Inquisition, held at the same time and place, before the aforesaid Justices, a different panel of jurors — some drawn from more distant places in Warwickshire — testified:

(9) That Thomas Malory, Knight, and four others [named] on June 4, 1451, extortionately took seven cows, two calves, a cart worth £4, and 335 sheep worth £22, of the goods and chattels of William Rowe and William Dowde of Shawell, co. Leicester, and carried them off to Newbold Revel.

One cannot help speculating as to the reason why, when one jury at Nuneaton had returned its verdicts on counts 1–8 of the indictment against Sir Thomas Malory, it should have been necessary to empanel another jury to hear evidence on an additional count, that relating to the forcible removal of cows and sheep from Shawell, co. Leicester, to Newbold Revel.

"In those days," says Dr. S. R. Gardiner, — referring to the case of Lord Molynes and John Paston, — "a jury was not to be trusted to do justice. In the first place it was selected by the Sheriff, and the Sheriff took care to choose such men as would give a verdict pleasing to the great men whom he wished to serve; and in the second place, supposing that the Sheriff did not do this, a juryman who offended great men by giving a verdict according to his conscience, but contrary to their desire, ran the risk of being knocked on the head before he reached home."

Chapter VII

BEFORE THE KING'S BENCH

WE HAVE to go to the Coram Rege Roll to find what next happened. There it is recorded that the Sheriffs of London were ordered to bring Sir Thomas Malory before the King at Westminster. "And having been asked, in reference to what had gone before, if he desired to be acquitted of the premisses, *he says that he is not in any wise guilty thereof, and for good or ill puts himself upon his country,* etc. And thereupon the said Thomas Malory was handed back to the said Sheriffs for safe custody until, together with the other causes," etc.

Had Sir Thomas refused to plead, it is worth remarking, he could not have been tried at all. According to mediæval law, a trial by jury could be held only with the consent of the accused; he must "*put himself* on the country." If he refused to plead, he could not be convicted, but the justices could keep him in prison and make life unbearable for him.

A curious point to be noted here — and one which seems highly significant — is that 24 jurors who were summoned at Westminster to try the case against Malory failed to answer their names. It is recorded that a levy was ordered to be made of their goods and chattels.

Another important fact to be observed is that when Sir Thomas died, in 1471, he was found to have no landed estate whatever, in spite of having inherited from his father manors in three countries. But when his widow died, nearly nine years later, she was credited with his patrimony. We are forced to the conclusion, therefore, that when Malory found himself prosecuted by the authorities, he protected the interests of his family by following the example of the monastic houses he had been attacking. "From a very early period the bishops and heads of religious houses, as one contrivance for evading the laws prohibiting alienations in mortmain, procured lands to be conveyed in fee simple to some friendly hand, upon trust that they and their successors should be permitted to enjoy the profits." [1] This contrivance, like others, was cut short by Parliament, and effectually as regards its original purpose; but it was quickly taken up by laymen, who perceived the extent and usefulness of its application. Assuming the feoffees to uses to be willing and faithful instruments of the beneficial owner, his advantages were great. Though he were involved in the civil strife of Lancaster and York, and dealt with as a traitor by victorious enemies, the land would be secured for his children; for it legally belonged not to him but to the feoffees to uses, and therefore was not forfeited by his attainder. [2]

A year elapses before we find the next reference. Then, on March 26, 1453, the Patent Rolls record a "Commission to Humphrey Duke of Buckingham, Edward Grey of Groby, Knight, [3] and the Sheriff of Warwick and Leicester, appointing them to arrest and bring before the King and Council Thomas Malorre,

---

[1] Spence, *Equitable Jurisdiction of the Court of Chancery.*

[2] Sir Frederick Pollock, *The Land Laws.*

[3] Lord of the manor of Lutterworth, he also held the title of Lord Ferrers of Groby. His son was the first husband of Elizabeth Woodville, afterwards Queen of Edward IV.

Knight, to answer certain charges." In view of the fact that the second member of the Commission was lord of the manor of Lutterworth, it appears likely that the offence or offences charged against Sir Thomas on this occasion related to Leicestershire. No information on the subject, however, is contained either in the King's Bench Indictments or in the Leicestershire Assize Roll for the period. "Divers Counties" likewise yielded nothing on this occasion.

Turning again to the Coram Rege Roll, we find that in 34 Henry VI, Sir Thomas Malory — who by this time had had experience of imprisonment in the Tower of London — was "by special grace of the Court" admitted to bail on the sureties of Sir Roger Chamberleyn, of Queenborough, Kent; John Hathwyk, Esq., of Harbury, Warwickshire; and other gentlemen. But if he gained his liberty, it was for a very short period.

The Coram Rege Roll tells us that in Hilary term, 34 Henry VI, a writ of "habeas corpora juratorum" was issued to compel the attendance of jurors to enquire if Thomas Malory, late of Fenny Newbold, Knight, "be guilty of divers felonies, transgressions, insurrections and extortions whereof he is indicted and not placed in respite before the lord the King."

On Friday next after the Feast of St. Hilary, 34 Henry VI, — in other words, January 16, 1456, — Sir Thomas was committed by the King's Bench to the custody of the Marshal. He had proffered letters patent showing that the King had pardoned him for all felonies and transgressions committed before July 9, 1455; but although several friends, including Roger Malory, of Ryton, Warwickshire, gentleman, offered to go bail for him, "Thomas Malory remains in the custody of the Marshal until sufficient security be found."

It is highly significant that nearly all the sureties proffered on the second occasion were of considerably less social standing than those named as being accepted in 32 Henry VI. Whereas a knight and six gentlemen from divers counties were willing to go bail in the first instance, in the second a London saddler and two tailors constituted one-half of the sureties — whom the Court deemed insufficient. The change in the situation makes it clear: (1) That Malory had been unable to curb himself during a short period of liberty granted to him; and (2) that he had alienated the support of men of his own rank and could now obtain sympathy only from that class which supplied the chief support of Lollardy. The attitude of London tradesmen in this respect is attested by Dr. James Gairdner and other historians. It is not suggested, of course, that Malory himself endorsed all the 24 Propositions which John Wycliffe advanced; the Knight of Newbold Revel must be regarded as a political rather than a doctrinal Lollard.

The refusal of the King's Bench at Westminster to release Malory in spite of his producing a Royal pardon recalls a parallel incident recorded to the credit of Sir John Fortescue, the Chief Justice at this period. A certain Thomas Kerver had been imprisoned for some offence in Wallingford Castle, when the King pardoned him and wished him to be released. But Fortescue, to whom the King sent a command to issue a writ for the purpose, considered that he had no right or legal power to do so, and refused to comply.

Towards the end of Henry VI's reign the Controlment Rolls contain further references to Sir Thomas Malory. From these we gather that, although he appears to have been in Warwickshire for a short time, he was again in prison in Hilary term, 38 Hen. VI. In Michaelmas term, 36 Hen. VI, it is recorded that Malory had been committed to the Marshalsea by the Chief Justice, Sir John Fortescue, "for divers causes pending before the King"; the Warwickshire Coroner, Thomas Greswold, is named also as a prosecutor of the Knight of Newbold Revel. Sir Thomas, meanwhile, was declared to be detained in prison by virtue of another writ of the King, of which the tenour was as follows:

Henry by the grace of God King of England & France & Lord of Ireland, to the Sheriffs of London Greeting. Because Thomas Malory, Knt., is detained in our prison of the Marshalsea for surety of the peace towards us & all our people, & especially towards the Abbot of Coombe & many others of our lieges, & for surety of good behaviour towards us & all our people, & for other causes specially moving us. We, for the greater surety of custody of the above-named Thomas, have committed the said Thomas to our prison of Newgate, to be kept safe & secure, Until we shall have ordered concerning him, & this under pain of 1,000 *li.* he shall not omit.

And now (continues the record), having learnt that the same Thomas is, for the reasons aforesaid, detained in our prison of Ludgate under your custody, we order & firmly enjoin you that you shall keep the aforesaid Thomas safe & secure for the causes aforesaid under the above-named penalty until you shall have order from us. Witnessed by J. Fortescu at Westminster on the 24th day of January in the 35th year of our reign.

Afterwards, on the Wednesday next after the 18th of Michaelmas this term, the aforesaid Thomas was delivered in bail to William Nevill Lord Fauconberge, William Briggeham of Briggeham in the county of York, Esq., & John Clerkson, of Arundel in the county of Sussex, Esq., until the morrow of St. John wheresoever etc, each of the pledges under pain of 20 *li.* & the aforesaid Thomas under pain of 400 *li.* under [?] etc. And for his good behaviour etc. On which day he appeared & was committed to the Marshalsea as well for the surety of the peace aforesaid as for his good behaviour etc. And also for the condemnation aforesaid etc. [*i. e.*, by the Warwickshire Coroner].

Afterwards, namely in Easter term in the 37th year of the said King's reign, the Court was informed by trustworthy men of the county of Warwick that the said Thomas was out of the custody of the said Marshal & had been at large in the county of Warwick since the feast of Easter in the said term of 37 (Hen. VI). Orders were thereupon given to the Marshal to keep the above-named Thomas Malory in the King's prison of the Marshalsea at Southwark in the County of Surrey & not permit the said Thomas to be at large outside the prison under pain of 100 *li*.

And afterwards, namely, in Hilary term in the 38th year of the said King's reign, the aforesaid Thomas Malory was committed to the custody of the Sheriff of Middlesex for reasons aforesaid, to be detained safe & secure in the King's prison of Newgate until etc. Therefore the said Marshall is discharged hereof etc.

Unfortunately the Controlment Roll for 39 Hen. VI is missing; and, the Rolls from 1 to 9 Edward IV do not mention Sir Thomas Malory so far as can be discovered. He does not seem to have been indicted in the reign of Edward IV, and the only further record to be discovered is his exclusion from the general pardon of 8 Ed. IV; but of course, as there are only two rolls for this period, he may have been excepted any time between the years 1 and 8 Ed. IV. It is certainly worthy of note that seven years after the attack on Coombe Abbey, it should be placed on record that Sir Thomas "is detained in our prison of the Marshalsea for surety of the peace towards us & all our people *and especially towards the Abbot of Coombe*." This, too, after Malory had produced the King's pardon for transgressions prior to 1455.

Chapter VIII

THE RAID ON COOMBE ABBEY

TWO things in particular are to be noted regarding the attacks on Coombe Abbey: that the first was made within twenty-four hours of Sir Thomas Malory's dramatic escape from the Sheriff's custody, and that the second attack came twenty-four hours later. That Malory should have renewed the assault in this way seems almost incredible; it may be that he was not personally concerned with the second attack, but was held responsible for it by the monastic authorities. Another theory, and probably the correct one, is that the two alleged attacks were one and the same affair. Once in possession of the Abbey during the Wednesday night, the rioters must have seized whatever Sir Thomas Malory claimed or they themselves fancied; there could have been no occasion to renew the attack on the following night. It would seem that we have here merely an instance of the regular legal fashion of describing the same offence, or parts of the same offences, in distinct counts. As Judge Parry humorously remarks of the old-style indictment: "How careful they were in the old days. One count of the Indictment would allege that the murderer was holding his knife in the right hand, another count thought it was his left, another alleged neither hand, and the last count always wound up by saying that the victim was murdered by means to the said jury unknown." [1]

[1] Judge Edward A. Parry, *What the Judge Thought*, p. 76.

But whatever may be the true explanation, the number and composition of Sir Thomas Malory's followers — yeomen, husbandmen, etc.[1] — prove that the Abbey was held in serious disfavour in the neighbourhood. Malory had only to apply the torch, in fact, to bring about an explosion. It is therefore well to see, if possible, what was the position of affairs at Coombe Abbey at this period. First of all, it has to be remembered that the time was one of stress for everybody, — "This was a-nother dere yere," commented a monastic chronicler in 1449, — and the strictness with which ecclesiastical corporations were accustomed to enforce their legal rights would naturally arouse resentment in some quarters. Serfdom in England, it is true, had received a mortal wound as the result of the Black Death and of Wat Tyler's Rebellion, but it lingered longest on ecclesiastical, and especially on monastic, estates. Evidence on this point is furnished by Sir Thomas Malory's own parish of Monks Kirby. Edward I had granted to the prior and convent of Kirkeby Monachorum "view of frankpledge with all that pertains to it . . . and infangtheof," and this grant was confirmed by Edward IV in 1469. "Infangtheof," it should be explained, was the right of doing justice to thieves apprehended on the lord's domain. What the manorial rights of Coombe Abbey were we may gather from the description Dugdale gives of those appertaining to another Cistercian monastery, that of Stoneleigh, a few miles distant. The custom was that "at the *Bederipe* in Harvest (*i. e.*, the general reap for the Lord's corn) the superior tenants (*sokemanni*) should all come upon request or notice with

[1] One of the raiders was a harpist, who came from Malory's own domain. The "bower" who also participated was evidently a maker of bows and arrows.

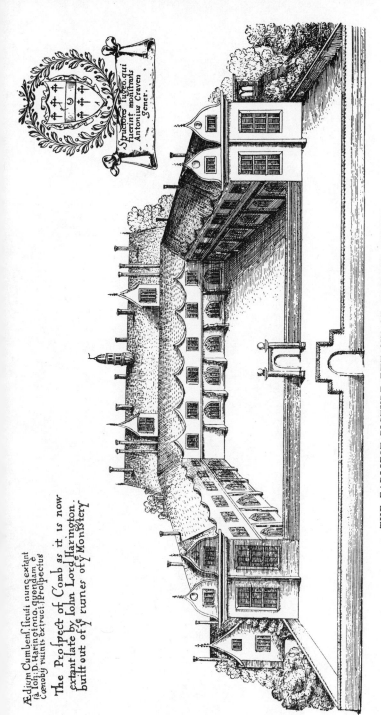

Ædium Cumbens: sicuti nunc extant (â Ioh: D. Harington.no. quondam e Cœnobij ruinis extruct:) Prospectus

The Prospect of Comb as it is now extant late by Iohn Lord Harington. built out of y̆ ruines of y̆ Monastery

Structora lugeo, qui fuerint monstrals Antonius Craven gener.

THE EARLIEST PICTURE EXTANT OF COOMBE ABBEY.

everyone of their tenants; the *sokemanni* to ride up and down on horseback, with wands, to see that they worked well, and to amerce those in the Court, then and there held, that made default or laboured idly. That they should be in the field at sunrising, and to work till sunset, not sitting down to breakfast, but each of them eating what he brought with him as they went up and down the lands to their work."

Passing from the general to the particular, we find in *Early Chancery Proceedings* the record of specific complaints made against the Abbot of Coombe at this time. To begin with, the tenants of "dame Katerine Reigne denglterre" at Brinklow complain that

Dan. Richard Atherston, Abbot of Coombe, would not allow the 15th granted to the King to be levied on his tenants. And when the complainants had taken distress the said Abbot strongly resisted, and they could not levy the 15th, to the great loss of the King. They ask for a writ of Appeal for the said Abbot to appear in Chancery, etc.

A curious complaint was that made by John Whalley of Coventry. He alleged that John Coton, "comoigne" to the Abbot of Coombe, had asked him to

take to farm of the said Abbot two messuages and two cottages in Bynley and a croft there called Dalby, for a term of years, paying yearly 38s. 4d., under certain conditions to be made in writing between the Abbot on one side and John Whalley on the other. By force of which John Coton gave the complainant a lease of the premises. The said John Whalley supposing the "licence of the said Comoigne had be lawfull and suffisaunt auctorite for hym to occupie," he entered the premises and for a year and more paid rent to the Abbot until the time that the Abbot and John Coton with one Richard Coventre, another of the monks, "ymagynyng to avoide the said suppliant of his said terme" and to deprive him of his goods and chattels, pretended that the complainant occupied the premises without lawful lease. They "cam to the said grounde and with their servaunts, v oxen price of everych xxs and v kyne price of everych of xiijs iiijd" of the complainant's "for damage fesaunt in the soill of ther house dref away and yet withholden" to the great damage of the complainant. He asks for a writ of subpœna, &c.

The aforesaid Richard, Abbot of Coombe, is next sued for "deffamacion" by John Shawe of Coventry and Joan his wife. Their complaint is that, in the absence of the said John,

the Abbot took from Joan without reason or course of law two horses worth 46s. 8d., one pack of wool . . . taffet cloth . . . sangweyn colour, another part of grene cloth worth 5s., two saddles and two bridles worth 13s. 4d., for the which heinous offences a writ of subpœna was directed to the Abbot to appear at Coventry, but he did not come. And the Abbot cited Joan twice to appear, and in her absence he and his counsel "token sentence oute of thearches,[1] of which sentence youre seid Oratrice hadde at that tyme no knowleche." By which the said Joan was imprisoned for 16. . . . Now the said Joan and her husband wish to sue the Abbot for "deffamacion."

"*Vi et armis*," it is quite clear, had become common form long before the phrase was employed to describe Sir Thomas Malory's conduct at Coombe Abbey on the night of July 23, 1451. But the Abbot's actions too could justify the use of the classic phrase, if we may judge by another petition addressed "to the Archbishop of Canterbury, Chancellor of England." In this

John Shawe of Coventry complains that Richard, Abbot of Coombe, with other persons unknown came with force and arms and at the same Abbey "on Wednesday before seint Gregorys day . . . certen goodes that is to wyte two horses

---

[1] Court of Arches?

worth 4 marks, 2 packs of [wool] worth 20s., 5 yards of wollen cloth worth 4s., 1 cloak worth 8s. 6d., 1 saddle and bridle 10s."

The rest is illegible except for a word here and there which do not help with the meaning.

It is curious, perhaps even significant, that the *Register de Cumba*, preserved at the British Museum, makes no reference whatever to the attacks on the Abbey in 1451. The monastic chronicler alludes to storms and battles, even finds space for a mathematical treatise, but of the dramatic events already referred to there is not the slightest mention.

How intriguing are the silences of history!

In the previous year the Abbot of Ramsey, in the County of Huntingdon, — a Benedictine monastery some fifty miles distant from Coombe, — made complaint of an assault by ninety men on his property, and obtained the appointment of a Commission of Oyer and Terminer to deal with the matter. It is conceivable that the attack led by Sir Thomas Malory was inspired by what happened on the occasion of the Huntingdon outbreak. The Abbot complained that ninety men (at the head of whom were an esquire, a "gentilman," and a bailiff) broke his closes and houses at Fenny Stanton and St. Ives, and the gates, doors and windows thereof; they cut certain cups and vessels to pieces and threw them into the river, and then broke a fountain and filled it to the top with dung and other refuse. Next they threatened Robert, prior of St. Ives, and John Alconbury,— the Abbot's fellow monks, — and the Abbot's tenants and servants in St. Ives, so that the prior fled to the bell-tower of the priory, and John Alconbury to a secret corner, and the rest of the monks to the Abbey of Ramsey. "And divers tenants dared not remain on the Abbot's land there, and his servants dared not go about his business." [1]

What the condition of affairs was at Ramsey Abbey about this time may be learned from the record of Bishop Alnwick's Visitation in 1439 (the last extant). It fully deserved the severe injunction uttered against Huntingdon Priory seven years previously by Bishop Gray: — "In our Visitation some time ago, by our right as Ordinary, of you and your priory, we found no good thing in the same which might be likened to religion, save only the outward sign. . . . The divine office, by night and likewise by day, is neglected; obedience is violated; the alms are wasted; hospitality is not kept. There is nothing else here but drunkenness and surfeit, disobedience and contempt, p^te aggrandise^t & apostasy, drowsiness — we do not say incontinence — but sloth & every other thing which is on the downward path to evil & drags men to hell."

The practice of land inclosure, which caused so much discontent in England, was just beginning at this time; but the monks of Coombe Abbey are not among the offenders named at the Parliamentary Inquiry of 1517. Neither is Monks Kirby mentioned in this connection. The Augustinian Priory of Kenilworth, on the other hand, is declared to have taken part in the inclosures.

[1] Patent Rolls.

Chapter IX

MONKS KIRBY: A TROUBLED HISTORY

IT WILL be observed that in the long indictment drawn up against Sir Thomas no mention whatever is made of any attack on monastic property at Monks Kirby — an "alien" house at this period assigned to the Carthusian Order at Axholme, Lincs. Yet it was because of a complaint from this source that the King's warrant to arrest Sir Thomas was issued on July 13, 1451, at Westminster. The warrant was directed to Humphrey, Duke of Buckingham, and Richard Neville, Earl of Warwick, and was couched in the following terms:

Know that for a few certain and notable causes set forth in our presence and the presence of our Council we have assigned you to take and arrest Thomas Malory, knight, and John Appelby, servant of the same Thos. Malory, wherever they may be found — as well within liberties as without — and to find sufficient mainpernors [sureties] who will be willing to give mainprise for them under good and sufficient penalty, to be enforced by you according to your reasonable discretion, that they, nor either of them, shall cause no injury or evil to the Prior and convent of the Carthusian Order of the Isle of Axholme or to any of our people, nor shall burn their houses, nor shall procure or cause the same in any way, and that the same Thomas Malory, knight, and John Appelby in their persons shall appear in our presence and the presence of the Council aforesaid on the quinzaine of Michaelmas next to answer upon those charges which shall there and then be preferred against them.[1]

---

[1] Patent Rolls.

The probable explanation is that the acts of extortion alleged against Sir Thomas Malory (see Nos. 6 and 9 of summarised Indictment) were made by him to recover possession of property taken on behalf of the Priory of Monks Kirby. This monastery had had a similar experience in the previous reign (Henry V's), for it is on record that the prior of Axholme had complained:

That William Colman, William Bosevyll, and Robert Fox have forcibly entered the priory of Monks Kirby and have taken away from the said suppliant the profits arising therefrom, and hold them against the proclamation lately made to the contrary. Different goods and chattels of great value, together with written charters and other muniments and £25 12s. 1d. in money belonging to the said suppliant there found, they also have taken and carried away. That it may please your Majesty and wise Council to ordain a remedy, considering that the said priory is the sustenance of the said suppliant and his convent.

It was probably the William Bosevyll above-mentioned who in 1401 at Nuneaton was excommunicated for "manifest contumacy in not obeying certain canonical monitions addressed to him."

The career of Monks Kirby Priory had indeed been troublous. As an "alien" house, — it was an offshoot of the Carthusian monastery of St. Nicholas, Angiers (the principal city of Anjou), — its revenues had of course been sequestered on the outbreak of the Hundred Years War. Sir Thomas Malory's grandfather had, in 1389, been a member of a Commission appointed "to enquire concerning the lands of the alien priory of Kirkby Monachorum, in the County of Warwick." What the result of their deliberations was we do not know; but seven years later Papal Letters show that complaint had been made that only two monks, instead of seven, resided at Kirby Priory (besides the prior); that the rule was not observed; and that on account of the dissolute life of the prior and French monks living there, and of their servants, who were at discord with the English, the buildings were partially falling. It was in consequence of this state of affairs that, at the instance of Thomas Mowbray, Duke of Norfolk, the priory was transferred to the Isle of Axholme, where he founded the important Carthusian monastery of Epworth. Scarcely had he done so when he was challenged to battle by the Earl of Hereford (afterwards Henry IV), and banished for life by Richard II. Claims for payment of tithe to a distant monastery were a fruitful source of discord at this period, and it seems likely that Sir Thomas Malory's "extortion" was in reality a form of reprisal.

Chapter X

THE MOST SERIOUS CHARGE AGAINST MALORY

TO MOST people, in our day, the gravest charge in the whole Indictment — and here Sir Thomas alone is concerned — is that in which he was accused of having twice violated the wife of Hugh Smyth of Monks Kirby, first at Monks Kirby, and then a couple of months later at Coventry. In one count, housebreaking and rape are alleged; in the next, rape and robbery — apparently from Smyth's house. Here again, however, Malory was probably merely seizing by violence goods and chattels to which he had (or said he had) some claim. The charge of *raptus* was doubtless merely incidental; it is very common in such cases, and often amounts to little more than a legal fiction, a formula used for good measure. Professor Kittredge thinks we may reconstruct events thus: "On May 23, 1450, Malory and his servants searched Smyth's house in vain. Smyth's wife, who objected to the search, may have been roughly treated; perhaps she was forcibly removed from the dwelling while it was ransacked. That would have been *raptus*. Then, on the first of August, the search was repeated with similar violence and with complete success, for goods and chattels valued (by Smyth!) at £40 were taken. On neither occasion is there any likelihood that Goodwife Smyth was actually ravished. The duplication of this particular charge is reason enough for rejecting such an idea: it is ridiculous to suppose that Malory actually ravished the woman twice. Anything, to be sure, is possible in what Sir Peter Teazle calls this 'damned wicked world,' but we are in pursuit of what is reasonable — and we are reading an indictment, not a verdict or the sentence of a judge."

"In *Chancery Proceedings*," writes Mr. C. L. Kingsford, "we hear so often of trespass committed by a number of persons unknown to the complainant but armed with all manner of weapons of war, that we are moved to suspect that the language is no more than the legal formula. Similarly, if the offence is that of the forcible abduction of a woman, we shall probably be told that when she was lying in her bed in God's peace and the King's, divers persons broke into her house and carried her away, clad only in her kirtle and smock. In both instances it was necessary to show that an offence had occurred of so serious a character as to call for the intervention of the Court of Chancery. If, as is so often the case, only the Bill of Complaint is preserved, we have no means to check the accuracy of the statements. When we have the defendant's Answer, a different complexion may probably appear." [1]

"In no wise guilty" was Sir Thomas Malory's plea when brought before the King's Bench in London a few months later, as we shall see.

The mediæval lawyers' liking for "piling on the agony" is well illustrated by the curious record which has come down to us of an earlier episode in Sir Thomas's career — a reference "not, perhaps, very much to his credit but sufficiently illustrative of those unruly times." (We quote Professor Kittredge.) It embodies

[1] *Prejudice and Promise in the XVth Century* (1925).

a charge of assault with violence which had been brought by Thomas Smythe, a parishioner of Sprotton, Northants, against Thomas Malory, *miles*, and another, in 1443; and the debased Latin of the De Banco Rolls is in this instance so picturesque that it must be quoted in all its legal verbosity:

(Northants). Thomas Smythe in propria persona sua optulit se quarto die versus Thomam Malory de parochia de Kirkeby monachorum in Comitatu Warw., militem, et Eustachium Burneby de Watford in Comitatu predicto, armigerum, de placito quare vi et armis in ipsum Thomam Smythe apud Sprottone insultum fecerunt et ipsum verberaverunt, vulneraverunt, imprisonaverunt, et male tractaverunt, et bona et catalla sua ad valenciam quadraginta librarum ibidem inventa ceperunt et asportaverunt, et alia enormia ad grave dampnum et contra pacem etc fecerunt. Et ipsi non venerunt, et preceptum fuit Vicecomiti quod attachiat eos, et Vicecomes modo mandat quod attachiati sunt per Richardum Gey et Johannem ffray.

It is worth recalling, in this connection, that the *Morte* tells us how King Arthur himself got into trouble on one occasion by paying a visit of inspection to La Belle Isoud before Sir Tristam had invited him to do so. Whereupon, Sir Launcelot (who accompanied the King) offered as a very proper and sufficient defence, that "it is every good knight's part to behold a fair lady."

Malory certainly affords no justification for the Tennysonian tradition of a priggish and vacuous Arthur who has nothing else to do but stalk about "wearing the white flower of a blameless life."

Still more to the point is it to quote the celebrated passage in which Malory likens true love to summer, his words forming a prelude to the tragic situation in which Launcelot is drawn this way by fidelity to his king, and

that way by fidelity to his mistress, whom he has to
rescue from the stake.

Like as herbs and trees bring forth and flourish in May, in
likewise every heart that is in any manner a lover, springeth
and flourisheth in lusty deeds. For it giveth unto every lover
courage, the lusty month of May, to constrain him to some
manner of thing more in that month than any other. . . .
Therefore like as May month flowereth and flourisheth in
many gardens, so in like wise let every man of worship flourish
his heart in this world, first unto God and next unto the Joy
of her that he promised his faith unto; for there was never
worshipful man nor worshipful woman, but they loved one
better than another; but first reserve the honour to God, and
secondly the quarrel must come of thy lady — and such love
I call virtuous love.

Further evidence on this point is to be found in Book
VI of the *Morte*, which tells how Sir Launcelot rode with
a damsel mounted on a white palfrey and slew a knight
that distressed all ladies.

Sir, said the damsel, here by this way haunteth a knight
that distresseth all ladies and gentlewomen, and at the least
he robbeth them or lyeth by them.
What, said Sir Launcelot, is he a thief and a knight and a
ravyssher of women?

As Dr. Oskar Sommer has pointed out in his monu-
mental work on the *Morte*, the words "ravyssher of
women" do not occur in the prose *Launcelot*, — Malory's
source-book for this particular section of his work, —
and it seems incredible that the knight of Newbold
Revel would have gone out of his way to mention this
crime if he had himself been guilty of it. Nor does
Malory confine himself to the words we have quoted.
The following passage, which has no counterpart in the
prose *Launcelot*, shows how deeply he detested conduct

that was dishonouring to women, and that was, moreover, expressly forbidden by the vows of knighthood. When Sir Launcelot is urged by the damsel to take a wife unto himself, he replies:

> To be a wedded man I think it not, for then I must couch with her, and leave arms and tournaments, battles and adventures. And as for to say for to take my plesaunce with paramours, that will I refuse in principal for dread of God. For knights that be adulterous, or wanton, shall not be happy nor fortunate unto the wars, for either they shall be overcome with a simpler knight than they be themselves, or else they shall by mishap and their cursedness slay better men than they be themselves. And so who that useth paramours shall be unhappy, and all thing is unhappy that is about them.

An equally emphatic passage is to be found in Book XI — and here again it is peculiar to Malory's version of the *Morte*. Sir Percivale, after rescuing a comrade-in-arms from the castle where he had been imprisoned by "an uncourteous lady" whose advances he had rejected, reproaches the dame in the following words:

> Ah, madam, said Sir Percivale, what use and custom is that in a lady to destroy good knights but if they will be your paramours? forsooth this is a shameful custom of a lady. And if I had not great matter in my hand, I should foredo your evil customs.

We do not know whom Sir Thomas Malory married except that her Christian name was Elizabeth and that she was evidently a woman of business capacity;[1] but after reading this we cannot help feeling that, whoever she was, she had a faithful husband, even if he was in the black books of the Cistercians and the Carthusians.

---

[1] The Reader MS. at Coventry contains the following (from the first Roll of the Pittancer, 1478–79): "To the servants of Lady Elizabeth Malory, bringing the Winwick rent, 1s. 8d." On the same page also appears: "To the Pittancer's servant riding to Winwick for the rent."

In this connection it is worth noting that Malory gives his wife's name to "king Mark's sister of Cornwall " — the mother of Sir Tristram. "She was called Elizabeth, that was called both good and fair . . . a full meek lady, and well she loved her lord" [king Meliodas]. Here Malory makes a definite alteration, for in the original Romance of Tristan the name of Meliodas's queen is "Isabelle." This is one of the few ladies in the *Morte* whose character is above reproach, — from a modern point of view, — and in bestowing on her the name of Elizabeth the knight of Newbold Revel was undoubtedly offering a compliment to his own spouse. Of both Elizabeths it could be said that they were deprived of the companionship of their husbands. The jealousy of another woman was responsible for the separation of Meliodas and his queen; whether Joan Smyth of Monks Kirby played the part of Potiphar's wife it is impossible to say.

Chapter XI

NOT AN ORDINARY FREEBOOTER

IT IS commonly supposed that in the Middle Ages the clergy — both Regular and Secular — were treated by the laity with profound respect, and that consecrated buildings in particular were kept inviolate. An examination of the facts does not bear out this supposition. We read in 1267 that the fine exacted for assaults on priests by men of knight's rank was £6 13s. 4d., — a substantial sum in those days, it is true, — but the fixing of a scale of fines for such offences tells its own tale. On one occasion alone the Papal nuncio received a faculty to absolve fifty persons who had laid violent hands on priests and clerks. Moreover, these assaults were sometimes perpetrated in sacred buildings, while services were being held.[1]

Warwickshire could furnish instances in point besides those already quoted. There were, in this county, two other Cistercian monasteries besides Coombe Abbey. In regard to Merevale Abbey we are told that, in 1292, John, son of John de Overton, brought a complaint against the abbot, four monks, and five brethren of the abbey, and others, for having caused the death of his brother Robert. Seven years later, John, probably in revenge, pulled down the abbot's house at Overton-by-Twycross, on the confines of the counties of Warwick

[1] A. Abram, *English Life and Manners in the Later Middle Ages.*

and Leicester, and carried away the timber by night.[1] Stoneleigh Abbey, the other Cistercian house, was in great trouble in the Spring of 1380, when malefactors seized the Abbey seal and used it to demise certain manors and granges and to grant certain pensions. They had also seized cattle, carried away books, chalices, vestments, jewels and other goods, and committed divers wastes.[2] It was, moreover, a descendant of the founder of Coombe Abbey who in 1418 was accused of leading an attack on the property of the Abbot of Evesham. Sir Thomas Burdett, of Arrow, was the Warwickshire knight against whom the complaint was made. It was asserted that, aided by his son Nicholas and other evil-doers, he broke into the Abbot's mill, put iron "pikkes" and "billes" between the mill-stones, and caused the mill to grind them — to the imminent peril of burning the mill-house. Not content with this, they hunted in the Abbot's warren and carried off 400 rabbits worth 10s. Nicholas Burdett had been a storm-centre five years earlier, when with 80 followers he had entered Shipston-on-Stour and wounded and ill-treated divers tenants of the Prior of Coventry, and killed certain tenants of the Prior of Worcester.[3] The number of assaults made on monasteries might surprise us, if we did not remember that these places, being corporate

---

[1] *Victorian County History of Warwickshire.*

[2] *Ibid.*

[3] When the two Burdetts finally appeared in Hilary Term, 1420, before the King's Bench, they were released on bail "pro eo quod ipsi profecturi sunt in partibus transmarinis in servitio dominis regis in Comitiva Johannis Ducis Bedeford." It seems clear that the King considered that men with the energy and courage to attack their fellow citizens could safely be employed in fighting the French. One is reminded of Pope Urban's plea: "Let those who for a long time have been robbers now become knights." — Miss B. H. Putnam, in *Early Treatises on the Practice of the Justices of the Peace in the 15th and 16th Centuries.*

bodies, had moved more slowly in the direction of emancipating their serfs than had the ordinary lord of the manor.[1]

We learn from the *Paston Letters* that in 1454 — shortly after Sir Thomas Malory was committed to prison — Robert Ledham's fellowship in Norfolk made an attack on two men while the latter were kneeling at Mass, and would have killed them had they not been prevented. The same year, two men beat the parson of Hashyngham, and "brake his hede in his own chauncell." Outrages like these were not the work of lawless brigands and recognised enemies of the whole community. They were merely the effect of party spirit. The men who did them were supported by noblemen and country gentlemen.[2]

What distinguishes Malory's case from that of a fomenter of disorder like Sir Thomas Todenham is that, whereas the latter is addressed by Richard Neville, Earl of Warwick (the King-Maker) as "our right trusty and well-beloved friend," [3] Malory incurs the displeasure of Red and White Rose supporters alike. Representatives of both factions are named on the Commission which arrests him; he is thrown into prison while the Lancastrians are in power; he is kept there when the Yorkists are in the ascendant. His views on the subject of civil war are expressed in Book X of the *Morte*, where, recounting how Sir Percivale delivered Sir Tristram out of prison, he interpolates the statement that King Mark had sworn

---

[1] G. M. Trevelyan.
[2] Dr. J. Gairdner's *Introduction to the Paston Letters.*
[3] In a letter written on All Souls' Day, 1449, "within our lodging in the Grey Friars within Newgate." The Earl was trying to negotiate a loan of money.

that he would go himself unto the Pope of Rome to war upon the miscreants. [Turks], and this is a fairer war than thus to raise the people against your king.[1]

Equally significant on this subject is another passage which Malory introduces in the account of Mordred's rebellion, when the people were "so new fangle" that for the most part they held with him

Lo ye all Englishmen, see ye not what a mischief here was, for he that was the most king and knight of the world, and most loved the fellowship of noble knights, and by him they were all upholden, now might not these Englishmen hold them content with him. Lo thus was the old custom and usage of this land. And also men say that we of this land have not yet lost ne forgotten that custom and usage. Alas this is a great default of us Englishmen; for there may no thing please us no term.

Moreover, Malory's "fellowship" included men of a higher social status than those who disturbed the peace in Norfolk. John Appelby, of Monks Kirby, who is given prominence as Malory's aider and abettor in the attacks on Coombe Abbey and Monks Kirby Priory, is described in the Indictment as "Esquire" and "gentil-man." He appears to have belonged to a family which "fetched its name" from Great Appleby in Leicester-shire,[2] and a member of which accompanied Wycliffe's protector, John of Gaunt, on his Spanish expedition.

Four yeomen and one husbandman, in addition to others of lower status, are named as having assembled with Malory "as rebels and breakers of the King's peace in the manner of an insurrection" and thereafter at-

[1] "On aperçoit ici une allusion aux événements politiques de l'époque, et notamment à la guerre des Deux Roses." — M. Eugène Vinaver, *Le Roman de Tristan et Iseut dans l'œuvre de Thomas Malory.*
[2] Fuller's *Worthies.*

tacked Coombe Abbey. The composition of Malory's "fellowship" recalls what a well-known historian has written about Jack Cade. "Cade was no leader of a second Peasant Rising. Among his followers were many yeomen, and not a few squires. Their grievances were not those of mere labourers, but of men of substance." [1]

It is very evident that Sir Thomas Malory, knowing he would be punished for what had happened at Monks Kirby, decided that he might as well "be hanged for a sheep as for a lamb." Nevertheless, he may have had no intention of going so far as he is declared by the Warwickshire jury's findings to have actually gone. But other popular leaders, before and since, have been carried off their feet by their followers; and particularly was this likely to be the case just after the close of the French Wars, when every county in England was disturbed by the presence of disbanded soldiery. We have it on record in Hardyng's Chronicle (1457) that:

> In every shire with jakkes [2] and salades [3] clene
> Myssereule doth ryse and maketh neyghbours werre.

Men of the type of Pistol were always ready to take advantage of any opportunity to commit robbery. Malory's effort to exact "wild justice" would give them the opportunity for which they were looking.

There is evidence, moreover, that men in a higher station of life brought home with them from France some of the manners they had acquired in the wars — manners more forcible than polite. A colleague of Sir Thomas Malory in the Retinue of the Earl of Warwick was Sir Thomas Lucy, of Charlecote. *Early Chancery*

---

[1] Sir J. H. Ramsay, *Lancaster and York*.
[2] Cuirasses.
[3] Open helmets.

Proceedings contain the "Complaint of Thomas Moston that Thomas Lucy of Charlecot in the county of Warwick, Gentleman, on the 25 of June last at Bishophampton with force and arms 'grevesly bette oon William Hewet' the complainant's servant 'thretyng hym to sle and to murder where he myght hym take where for he durst nought a byde to do shiche service' to the plaintiff 'as he hadde made his covenant to do atte his maner of Hontescote yn husbondrie and chargit other servauntes of your forsaid suppliant to voide froo his said maner and froo his service uppon the payne of deth' — which was greatly to the plaintiff's hurt because no one was there to look after 'suche good as God hath sende hym and may have noo servant a bydyng atte the said maner to gette ony frute beying upon the yerthe for drede of dethe.' He asks for a writ of subpœna to be issued to the aforesaid Thomas Lucy."

To regard the Knight of Newbold Revel as an ordinary freebooter is quite impossible in view of what we know about him. He had "a stake" not only in one county but in three. From his father and grandfather he had inherited his manors in Warwickshire, Leicestershire, and Northamptonshire. The right of presentation to the living of Shelton, Lincs., was also in his gift. When his widow died in September, 1479, leaving a 14-year-old grandson, Nicholas, as heir, it was placed on record that the property at Wynwyck which she held in chief was worth £10 per annum; the Newbold Revel manor, £6 13s. 4d.; the manor of Swynford, Leicestershire, four marks a year; and land at Stormefield, in the same county, 26s. 8d. yearly.

Sir Thomas Malory was not the only member of his family at loggerheads with the authorities. In 1454, a near relative, John Poultney, lord of the manor of Misterton (adjoining Lutterworth), — "a member of a family usually conspicuous for loyalty to Church and State," [1] — was accused before Bishop Chedworth "for refusing to pay tithes, withdrawing from confession and divine service, inciting others to do the like, and uttering divers speeches against the Christian faith." Poultney, however, recanted. It is significant, nevertheless, that when Sir William Peyto, Kt., of Chesterton,[2] co. Warwick, was in the Marshalsea prison, a year later, Poultney secured his release by giving surety for his good behaviour. The tendency for "birds of a feather" to flock together would seem to be further illustrated by the fact that Poultney's son married a daughter of the Lucys of Charlecote, where later (in 1545) Fox the Martyrologist was engaged as tutor.

It is to be hoped that during his long captivity Sir Thomas Malory derived some small share of benefit from the 53s. 4d. which John Poultney's great-grandfather, Sir John Poultney — five times Lord Mayor of London — had by his will left annually to the prisoners in Newgate. Malory, one imagines, must have been kept in touch with his native shire by the fact that the London residence, of the Earl of Warwick adjoined Newgate. The tables in the neighbourhood of Warwick's inn were full of meat which visitors were allowed to carry off from the Earl's hospitable abode.[3] Indirectly, therefore, the prisoners near by would stand to benefit.

[1] Leicestershire County Victoria History.
[2] It was at Chesterton that Sir John Oldcastle had lain concealed as a fugitive in Henry V's reign.
[3] Stow's *Chronicle*.

Chapter XII

NEWGATE GAOL. THE LONDON LIBRARY

NEWGATE GAOL, to which Sir Thomas Malory
was finally committed, — after periods of confinement in the Tower of London, Ludgate Prison, and
the Marshalsea, — was used at this period as a place of
detention both for prisoners of State and for ordinary
criminals. One offender of the same category as Sir
Thomas had just been released from there, namely,
William Wyghall, of Nottingham, yeoman, who "for
certain offences against the cathedral Church of St.
Peter, York, and John, cardinal and archbishop of that
church," had been committed to Newgate. Wyghall,
however, having "merited the benefit of absolution by
the cardinal," had on February 20, 1452, received pardon "for all felonies, murders, escapes, and all other
offences and any consequent outlawries." As the Bas-
tille of the day, Newgate was an object of popular
wrath during Wat Tyler's Rebellion, — it is recorded
that "the mob brake up the prison of Newgate," — and
it was rebuilt partly, if not wholly, at the expense of
Lord Mayor Richard Whittington, a "Warwickshire
lad," [1] who passed to his reward some 25 years before

[1] Long Compton, on the Gloucestershire border, claims to have been his
birthplace. "Dick Whittington's cottage" is in the village. The superior
claim of Pauntley, Glos., is based on an admittedly incorrect assumption.
See Mr. F. Were's article in the Bristol and Gloucestershire Archæological
Society's *Proceedings*, vol. xxxi, p. 286. This was published in 1908, but the
makers of Gloucestershire guide-books still gaily repeat the error.

Sir Thomas Malory's arrival in London to await the King's pleasure. Not only had Whittington provided for the secure government of the city, however. He exemplified the new interest in literature by founding what was in fact the first city Library — this on the premises of the Grey Friars, just across the road. He laid the first foundation-stone on October 21, 1421 (the Feast of St. Hilary), and in three years the building — which was 129 feet long and 31 feet broad — was filled with books, costing £556 10s., "whereof Richard Whittington gave £400." [1]

It is unfortunate that the records of the London Grey Friars Library do not specify the volumes which it contained; but we know, from other sources, that monastic institutions were well provided with the literature Malory would find essential when compiling the *Morte*. Book V of his work, for example, is compiled from *La Morte Arthure*, an English metrical romance of which a copy has been found in the Thornton MS. in Lincoln Cathedral Library.[2] The Abbey Church of St. Augustine in Canterbury, in the 15th century, had a library that contained about 1,900 volumes, ". . . also the romances of *Guy of Warwick*, *The Knight of the Swan*, *Lancelot du Lac*, *The Story of the Graal*, and the *Four Sons of Aymon*." [3] The Dover Priory library contained 450 books, including *Le Romaunt de la Rose* and *Le Romaunt de Roy Charlemayne*.[4] "The Friers of All Orders, and chiefly the Franciscans, used so diligently to procure Monuments of Literature from all Parts, that wise Men looked upon it as an Injury to Lay Men,

[1] Dugdale's *Monasticon*.
[2] *Dictionary of National Biography*, Article on Malory.
[3] H. R. Plomer, *Wm. Caxton*.   [4] *Ibid*.

LONDON'S FIRST LIBRARY, NEAR NEWGATE GAOL.

who therefore found a difficulty to get any Books." [1]
To like effect, but in a different tone, is the testimony
of Richard of Bury: "When I happened to turn aside to
towns and places where the Mendicants had their con-
vents, I was not slack in visiting their Libraries. There,
amidst the deepest poverty, I found the most precious
riches treasured up." [2]

Sir Thomas Malory was neither the first nor the last
inmate of Newgate to indulge in literary activity there.
Eleven years before the Warwickshire knight's arrest,
Charles, Duke of Orleans, had been released from Newgate after a captivity in various English strongholds ex-
tending over a quarter of a century. [3] He had whiled
away the dreary hours writing ballads and rondels; but
besides confirming himself as an habitual maker of
verses, he was a celebrated bibliophile, and had vied
with his brother Angoulême in bringing back the library
of their grandfather Charles V, when the Duke of Bed-
ford put it up for sale in London. [4] It is impossible to
doubt that he, too, found the proximity of the Grey
Friars Library most useful. When released by the English Government, — who hoped that he would go home
and stir up discord at the French Court, — he retired to
his palace at Blois, which became famous as the centre
of one of the most literary and polite societies of his
time. [5]

The extent to which Newgate was used as a place of
detention for State prisoners, as well as those convicted

[1] *Monasticon.*
[2] *Philobiblon,* c. 8.
[3] Taken prisoner at Agincourt, he had since been held in close custody in
England.
[4] Champollion-Figeac.
[5] Kenneth H. Vickers, *Humphrey Duke of Gloucester.*

of felony, is further indicated by the fact that John, Duke of Bourbon, another captive of Agincourt, spent 18 years within its walls and died there, being afterwards buried in the church of the Grey Friars.

To Malory, as he reduced into English the many French MSS telling the story of King Arthur and the Knights of the Round Table, the existence of the Library so near at hand must have been a veritable godsend during his long detention. "Detention," indeed, expresses his situation much more accurately than incarceration: for had he been confined in the fetid dungeons which Newgate possessed, his life would have been as short as those of the Carthusians who, being imprisoned for refusing to acknowledge the supremacy of Henry VIII, succumbed in a few weeks to their loathsome surroundings.

Although unable to secure his freedom, Malory would be able through his wife and family to purchase various concessions from the Governor of Newgate Gaol — a recognised procedure in the Middle Ages and for centuries later. We find, for example, in December, 1448, a grant for life of the "appurtenances, wages, fees, and profits" of the County Gaol at Warwick to Thomas Trueblode as a reward for good services in France and Normandy.[1] Except in the worst cases, most prisoners were able to ameliorate their condition by money. The gaoler looked on his prisoners as a type of paying guest, and the more they paid, the less irksome became their confinement. "The sums paid to gaolers naturally varied very much according to the prisoner. The Earl of Surrey paid the great sum of 40s. per week for himself, and 2s. 6d. per week for each of his men." [2]

[1] Patent Rolls.   [2] W. G. Bell's *Great Fire of London*.

Malory's captivity, then, was not without alleviation. But when all is said, he must have known little liberty for nearly twenty years. "We may talk very wisely of alleviations; there is only one alleviation for which the man would thank you: he would thank you to open the door."[1] Years after, when Charles of Orleans was speaking at the trial of the Duke of Alençon, who began life so hopefully as the boyish favourite of Joan of Arc, he sought to prove that captivity was a harder punishment than death. "For I have had experience myself," he said, "and in my prison of England, for the weariness, danger, and displeasure in which I then lay, I have many a time wished I had been slain at the battle where they took me."[2]

What would Malory not have given to wet his boots once more with morning dew and join in the chase over those grassy expanses in Warwickshire and Leicestershire which still form the best hunting countries in England?

An event heralding the Wars of the Roses must have come under Malory's notice in 1457, for the monotony of life in prison was broken by the arrival of Lord Egremond, a member of the Northumbrian House of Percy, who had been involved in a miniature civil war at Stamford Bridge despite the royal warning to be "sad, a sober, and a well-rewl'd man." We may be sure that this year would stand out in Sir Thomas Malory's memory, for Lord Egremond, soon after his arrival at Newgate, "brake out of prison by night and had a horse ready and rode away and one of the jaylers with him." [Three years later he was slain with the Duke of Buckingham

[1] R. L. Stevenson, *Essay on Charles of Orleans.*
[2] Champollion-Figeac.

close to the King's tent at Northampton.] The other prisoners took to the leads of the gate and defended it a long while against the Sheriffs and all their officers, insomuch that they were forced to call more aid of the citizens, whereby they lastly subdued them and laid them in irons.[1]

Bearing in mind Sir Thomas's past record as a prisonbreaker, it is highly probable that he too tried to escape on this occasion.

[1] Loftie.

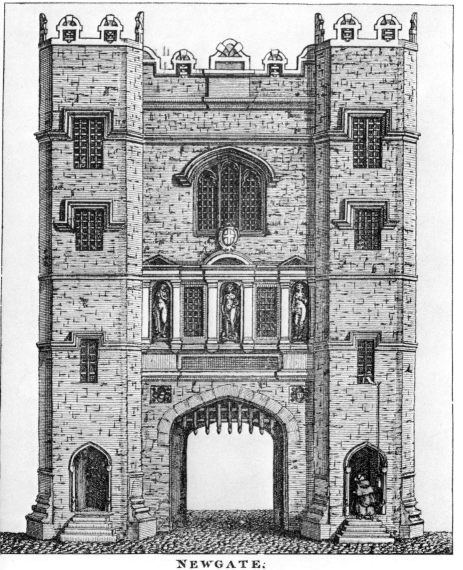

NEWGATE:

MALORY'S LAST PLACE OF DETENTION.

Chapter XIII

AMONG THE UNPARDONABLES

THE year before he finished the *Morte*, "Thomas Malorie, miles," was with other gentlemen excluded from a pardon granted to a large number of Edward IV's subjects;[1] and four months later, when practically the same list was again promulgated, "Thomas Malarie, knight," was again one of those excluded from the amnesty, granted "tylle alle manere of men for all manere of insurrecyons and trespasses."[2] Much water had flowed under the bridges since the Inquisition presided over by Duke Humphrey was held at Nuneaton. The Duke himself had fallen in battle at Northampton (in 1460), fighting on the Lancastrian side, and any offence which Sir Thomas Malory had committed against him would not weigh with the Yorkists who were now in power. As a matter of fact, Duke Humphrey's overthrow was the signal for Malory's friend, Sir Baldwin Mountford, to press his claim to the manor of Coleshill, of which after his father's death in 1453 he had been unjustly deprived by the Duke. Emerging from the ecclesiastical sphere in which he had taken refuge, he now published "a particular Instrument, whereunto he set his Hand and Seal," in which he made manifest "what unjust and ill-dealing had been exercised by the before-specified Duke of Buckingham for

[1] Wells register (*Hist. MSS Comm. 10th Report*, App. iii, 184).
[2] *H. M. C. Wells MSS*, i, 407.

the utter disheriting of him and his Son. . . . 'For in
trouth the seid Duke keped me in Coventre xiiii deyes,
and after had me to the Castell of Maxstoke, and there
kept me: And my son Sir Symond was put in the Castell
of Gloucester, and we could never be delivered out, till
we agreed to certain Articles written in a Bill anexid to
this my writinge.' " [1]

How Sir Thomas Malory was regarded by the authorities in 1468 is seen by observing the names which
preceded and followed his in the list of "unpardona-
bles." The first-named offender, Sir Humphrey Ne-
vyll, shared the Lancastrian sentiments of the elder
branch of his house. After Towton he was captured
and attainted; but later, breaking out of the Tower, he
returned to Northumberland and "made a commotion
of people against our sovereign lord the king." After
sueing for pardon, he was knighted, but again took arms
with the Lancastrians and lived the life of a freebooter
for five years. His attainder was now revived, and when
he was again captured he was executed at York (September, 1469) in the presence of King Edward IV.[1]
After Sir Thomas Malory's name came that of "Robert
Marshall, gentleman," who in 1465 had escaped from
prison at Nottingham, thus causing the sheriff of the
county to be liable to a penalty of 500 marks, from which
he was excused by royal clemency.[2]

Further proof that Malory died under a cloud is
found in the Record of *Inquisitiones post mortem*. He
had, as we have seen, inherited from his father landed
estates in Warwickshire, Leicestershire, and Northamptonshire; but after his death, in March, 1471 (1470, Old
Style), the customary Inquisitions were not held in

[1] Dugdale.   [2] *Dictionary of National Biography.*

Warwickshire or Leicestershire; and that which was
held in Northamptonshire — on November 6 — declared that he held neither lands nor tenements in that
county. We learn from the Northampton Inquisition,
however, that his son Robert — his heir — was 23
years of age at this time, a fact which may possibly help
us to fix the date of Sir Thomas's marriage. (It does not
at all follow, as we have suggested in a footnote on this
page, that Robert was the only son of the marriage.)
Robert's death, in 1479, caused a commission to be
issued to Walter Mauntell, knight, and two others, "to
enquire what lands Robert Malory, esquire, deceased,
tenant-in-chief, held in Northamptonshire, Warwickshire and Leicestershire." [1] Soon afterwards Sir Thomas's widow passed away, — eight and a half years after
her husband's death in Newgates, — and it is then that
we find full record of the manors, etc., which were now
recognised as being the property of Sir Thomas's grandson, Nicholas. The latter, it is worthy of note, lived to
become High Sheriff of Warwickshire and Leicestershire
in 18 Henry VII, thus retrieving the position in county
life which Sir Thomas had forfeited. [2]

[1] Calendar of Patent Rolls, 1476–85, p. 183.
[2] Nicholas Malory was succeeded by two daughters, one of whose descendants is Lord Braye. Newbold Revel passed into other hands in 1640,
and the site of the old manor house is now occupied by a mansion of the
period of Queen Anne. It was from an uncle or brother of Nicholas Malory,
probably, that "Master Melchisedech Mallerie" traced his descent. This
Melchisedech — described as "of a good spryte, ready tonge, in audacitie
forward" — came much into public notice in 1573, when with drawn sword
he chased a certain Arthur Hall through the streets of London, and a short
time afterwards was himself slain. In the legal proceedings which followed,
mention is made of the fact that Melchisedech's personal friends were Edward Grevill[e] and Sir John Conway — both prominent Warwickshire names,
— the latter at that period being connected with Monks Kirby. (*Miscellanea
Antiqua Anglicana*, 1815.) "In audacitie forward": there can be little doubt
whence Melchisedech Mallerie inherited this trait of his character.

Chapter XIV

MALORY'S BURIAL-PLACE

WHEN I am dead, I pray you all pray for my soul," wrote Sir Thomas Malory as he laid down his pen on finishing the *Morte*. His great task was completed some time between March, 1469, and March, 1470, and just over a year later — in March,[1] 1471 — he died. His death was probably due to the plague, for Sir John Paston tells us that in 1471 there was a terrible outbreak, "the most unyversall dethe that evyr I wyst in Ingelonde." Less than a fortnight after Malory had passed away, Edward IV landed at Ravenspur and, marching *via* Leicester, Coombe Abbey, Coventry and Warwick, overthrew the King-Maker at Barnet. The King, however, had taken such fright that, before the danger from the Lancastrians was past, he swallowed ten pounds' worth of medicine, "contra pestem" (Issue Roll, 15 May).

Malory's body found sepulture in the Grey Friars' sanctuary. "In Capella Sancti Francisci" — so ran the record of the event — "sub 2ª parte fenestre 4ᵉ sub lapide jacet dominus Thomas Mallere, valens miles: qui obiit 14 die mensis Marcij Aº dni 1470, de parochia de Monkenkyrkby in comitatu Warwici." [2]

The epithet "valens," inscribed on Sir Thomas Malory's tombstone of marble, may be translated "worthy"; but its value as evidence that the Grey Friars held him

---

[1] The inscription on his tombstone stated "Mch 14"; but according to the *Inq. pm* the date was March 12.   [2] Cotton MS., Vitellius.

in esteem is discounted by the fact that they applied
the same adjective to Nicholas Brembre, a Lord Mayor
of London, who was hanged at Tyburn in 1388 and whose
body was interred in the adjacent chapel of All Saints.
"Valens armiger," too, was said of Thomas Burdett,[1] of
Arrow, in the county of Warwick, who after his execu-
tion for high treason in 1477 was buried alongside
Brembre.

But the Grey Friars — "the Salvation Army of the
Middle Ages," as Miss Dormer Harris (the well-known
historian of Coventry) has termed them — could not
have maintained the splendour of their sanctuary merely
by interring those who had rendered themselves amen-
able to the law. "There were buried in this monastery
four queens, two daughters of kings, and almost innumerable earls, countesses, barons, bishops, and of the
better sort of citizens."[2] There was a reason for this
preference of a spot so close to "Stynkyng Lane."[3]
The Grey Friars' churchyard was thought to be pecul-
iarly free from evil spirits and flying demons of all sorts.[3]
As was to be expected, the Grey Friars utilised this idea
to enrich their establishment. After the manner of dogs,
declared Thomas de Walsingham, they greedily ate up
those who had become corpses. "You see he writes
somewhat passionately of the poor Friers: but consider
that he was himself a Monk, and the reason may easily
be discerned."[4]

To the Friars, who were very well aware of the light
in which the Monks regarded them, it must have been

[1] Enraged at Edward IV's action in killing a favourite white buck belonging to himself, Burdett passionately wished the horns in the King's belly.
For this he was convicted of high treason.

[2] *Monasticon.*

[3] W. Thornbury, *Old and New London.*   [4] *Monasticon.*

no small satisfaction to reflect that Sir Thomas Malory, *Malleus Monachorum*, had found a resting-place in their precincts; and probably — if the truth were known — had made a bequest, both of money and MSS, to those whose Library had been his help and solace during long years of captivity.

Malory's body reposed under a marble in the Grey Friars' Chapel until the Reformation (less than a century later), when Henry VIII ordered the sanctuary to be handed over to the Lord Mayor and burgesses of London for civic purposes. Malory's tombstone was one of "seven score all sold for £50 or thereabouts" by Sir Martin Bowes, Lord Mayor in 1545. "St. Bartholomew's Spittle (Hospital) in Smithfield, this Church of the Grey Friars, and two parish churches, the one of St. Nicholas in the Shambles, and the other St. Ewin's in Newgate Market, were all to be made into one parish in the said Friers Church . . . and called Christ's Church, founded by King Henry VIII. *A very odd Foundation to let two Churches of four stand, subverting the other two, and a good Hospital, and to call himself a Founder. . . .* Thus was a beautiful church defaced by sacrilegious hands." [1]

Scarcely had Sir Thomas Malory died when another Midland knight was also brought a prisoner to Newgate. This was Sir Walter Wrottesley, who, after being pardoned in 1471 for holding Calais against King Edward IV, was seized and imprisoned for debt. He died on April 10, 1473, and, like Malory, was buried in the church of the Grey Friars. "Miles strenuus in armis cum comite Warwici" was the epitaph granted to him — an epitaph defective in grammar and inaccurate in fact, seeing that really he belonged to Staffordshire.

[1] *Monasticon.*

Chapter XV

DID THE WARWICKSHIRE KNIGHT WRITE THE *MORTE*?

IT WILL be asked, How can it be proved that Sir Thomas Malory, Kt., of Newbold Revel, Warwickshire, was the author of the *Morte d'Arthur?* The answer is, He is the only one who fulfils the conditions, which are: (1) He must have been a knight; (2) he must have been alive in the ninth year of Edward IV — March 4, 1469, to March 3, 1470 (both included); (3) he must have been old enough in 9 Edward IV to make it possible that he should have written this work. Further, Caxton does not say that he received the "copy" directly from the author, and his language may be held to indicate that Malory was dead when the book was printed. In this case, he must have died before the last day of July, 1485, and we have a fourth condition to be complied with.

All these conditions (including the fourth, which can hardly be regarded as imperative) are satisfied by Sir Thomas Malory of Newbold Revel, and by none other. Professor Kittredge has dealt very exhaustively with this question, and his conclusion is as follows: "No one need hesitate to identify 'Thomas Malorie, miles,' of this (1468) pardon with the Warwickshire gentleman whom we are now considering. There appears to have been but one Sir Thomas Malory, Kt., living in England in 8 Edward IV. . . . This leaves, so far as appears at present, the Warwickshire Sir Thomas in possession of the field, for out of all the families examined in the present investigation, he is the only person found who fulfils the conditions of the problem."

The present writer, who has searched the *Inquisitiones post mortem* of the period and made other genealogical researches, can corroborate Professor Kittredge's testimony. It is a curious fact that in the very year in which the writer of the *Morte* finished his great work (that is, the ninth year of Edward IV's reign), the estate of Thomas Malory, *armiger*, of Kent, came up for probate — to use a well-understood phrase. But Caxton, in his introduction to the *Morte*, quite definitely says that this book was written by "Sir Thomas Maleore, knight." In any case, Thomas Malory, *armiger*, must have died prior to this, otherwise his name would not occur when it does in the *Inquisitiones post mortem*.

Shortly after the appearance of Professor Kittredge's essay (1897), Mr. A. T. Martin, F.S.A., read a paper before the Society of Antiquaries in which he discussed the claim of Thomas Malory of Papworth to be considered as the author of the *Morte d'Arthur*. This Malory did not die till the autumn of 1469; hence he was alive at the time when the *Morte* was finished, and possibly for six months afterwards. In the Fine Roll of Edward IV (1469, November 18) he is called "armiger," however, and this, combined with the fact that his will contains no designation of rank, makes it certain that he did not write the *Morte*.

Another Thomas Malory of this period ought perhaps to be mentioned before passing on to another point. In the list of noblemen and gentlemen who accompanied Edward IV in his northern expedition in 1462 appears the name of "Thomas Malery," and as it is included among the *milites* there may seem strong reason for regarding this Thomas as fulfilling the conditions just enumerated. When the list is examined closely, however, it becomes quite certain that this warrior against the Scots was not the Malory with whom we are concerned. "Sir" is prefixed to the name of each individual knight in the list, and the "Thomas Malery" here mentioned has no such prefix.[1]

"We cannot tell when, or, very distinctly, where, Caxton set up the first English press; he was too busy" (to mention this), said Bishop Stubbs in his "Lectures on Mediæval and Modern History." A very different reason is assigned by a present-day writer, namely, that Caxton, in introducing printing, was running counter to a sort of trade-union interest — that of the men who earned their living by copying MSS.[2] We may be certain that Caxton, when he acquired what Malory had "drawn out into English," knew that the author had died in prison under a cloud; but in the interests of the book he was about to publish,[3] the Father of English printing would naturally refrain from saying anything as to the career of the man whose great work he was giving to the world.

Giving our attention now to the internal evidence, — that presented by the *Morte* itself, — we find at least three instances in which Malory contrived to introduce complimentary references to names possessing a special Warwickshire significance. In Book II, where he tells of the prowess of King Arthur against Nero and King Lot of Orkney, he says: "Sir Hervis *de Revel* did mar-

[1] *Three Fifteenth-Century Chronicles*, ed. Gairdner, p. 157.
[2] H. R. Plomer.
[3] Caxton finished printing the *Morte* on July 31, 1485.

vellous deeds with King Arthur." When the question
of filling vacancies amongst the knights of the Round
Table is being considered (Book IV), "Sir Hervise de
Revel, *a noble knight*," is suggested by King Pellinore
as one of the four senior candidates. "That is well devised, said King Arthur, and right so shall it be." In the
source from which Malory took Books I–IV, viz., Robert
de Borron's "Romance of Merlin," Sir Hervis indeed
has a surname — "de Rinel"; but whilst it is unsafe to
attach much importance to Malory's constant changing
of this to "Revel," it is certainly significant that he introduces complimentary references to Sir Hervis de
Revel which are not to be found in "the frensshe book."
The names of the other candidates, it should be observed, are recited by Malory as given in the "Merlin"
— without any complimentary addition of his own.
Tasso and Ariosto, among Malory's contemporaries,
furnish proof of the practice in which fifteenth-century
authors indulged of introducing bits of personal and
family history into their works; and when we consider
the high value which descendants of the Revells set upon
their connection with that family, it is natural that we
should attach importance to the piece of evidence just
cited. How prominent was the Revell name in fifteenth-
century Warwickshire is made clear by a number of
facts. First of all, the place of Sir Thomas Malory's
birth was tending to be known as Newbold Revel rather
than as Fenny Newbold. Secondly, the Revell coat-of-
arms is encountered in a considerable number of parish
churches — or rather, this was so when Sir William
Dugdale compiled his "Antiquities of Warwickshire."
For example, it was the Revell coat-of-arms which
adorned one of the windows at Grendon, where Sir

Thomas Malory's father, John Malory, *armiger*, had married Philippa Chetwynd, daughter of a family which held a leading position in North Warwickshire as well as at Ingestre, in Staffordshire. Moreover, the Revell cognisance appeared four times in the chancel windows at Coleshill, — a place now, for us, always associated with Sir Thomas Malory's prison-breaking, moat-swimming achievement, — and it is still retained at Stanford-on-Avon Church (near Winwick) in the central window of the south aisle. Finally, we read that in 1408, Richard Reynolds, of Emscote, co. Warwick., "affecting his mother's name, called himself Revell."

Let us turn now to another and similar point. When we remember that Malory's feudal chief, Richard Beauchamp, besides being Earl of Warwick, claimed the barony of De Lisle in right of his wife, and that the title was revived in 1443 in favour of the Earl's grandson, John Talbot, Earl of Shrewsbury,[1] we cannot help recalling the important and highly honourable position which a knight bearing that surname occupies in the pages of the *Morte*. We read (Book XIII) how Galahad, after meeting Joseph of Arimathea, was by a monk brought to a tomb.

Anon, the squire [Melias de Lile] alight off his hackney, and kneeled down at Galahad's feet, and prayed that he might go with him till he had made him knight.
If I would not refuse you?
Then will ye make me knight, said the squire, and that order, by the grace of God, shall be well set in me.
So Sir Galahad granted him, and turned again unto the

---

[1] Slain with his heroic sire at Chatillon in 1453. The Patent Roll of 1450 mentions the "appointment for life of John Talbot, lord of Lysle, as master of the game of Fulbrooke Park, co. Warwick, together with the lordship and manor of Fulbrooke."

abbey there they came from. . . . And upon the morn he made
the squire knight, and asked him his name, and of what kin-
dred he was come.

Sir, said he, men call me Melias de Lile, and I am the son
of the king of Denmark.

Now, fair sir, said Galahad, sith ye be come of kings and
queens, now look that knighthood be well set in you, for ye
ought to be a mirror unto all chivalry.

Sir, said Melias, ye say sooth. But, sir, sithen ye have made
me a knight, ye must of right grant me my first desire that is
reasonable.

Ye say sooth, said Galahad.

Then Melias said, that ye will suffer me to ride with you in
this quest of the Sancgreal till that some adventure depart us.

I grant you, sir.

Reference to the source from which Malory drew this
particular portion of the *Morte,* viz., the French "Romance of Lancelot," shows that it contains no mention
whatever of "de Lile." Melias there is pure "Melian"
or "Meliane," with no surname. Nor indeed is the fan-
ciful description of Melias as "the son of the King of
Denmark" to be found in "the frensshe book." Instead
we find this:

> *Et chil li dist qu'il auoit a non melian, "biaus amis," fait
> galaad, "puis ke vous estes chivalers,* ET DE SI HAUTE LIGNIE
> COMME DE ROY, *ore gardes bien que li hounours de chevalerie
> soit bien emploie en vous."*

The position of Deputy Captain of Calais was held
for a time at this period by Sir William de Lisle. In the
light of this fact it is interesting to note that Malory
makes one of Sir Launcelot's knights, Nerovens de Lile,
lieutenant of the Castle of Pendragon. Nothing whatever suggestive of this is to be found in the source-book
which Sir Thomas Malory had before him when he
wrote, so that it is reasonable to suppose he in this way

wove into the *Morte* a bit of the history of his own time. As in the case already cited, however, he half conceals while he half reveals. Here his method is fully in accord with that of earlier writers in the Arthurian Cycle.

Book XVIII furnishes us with a noteworthy example of Malory's habit of giving distinctive appellations to persons who in "the frensshe books" were nameless. When Sir Launcelot is dangerously wounded by accident at the hand of his friend Sir Bors, he pleads to be taken to the dwelling-place of "a gentle hermit, that sometime was a full noble knight and a great lord of possessions, . . . and his name is Sir Baudewin of Bretayne." Malory knew a Sir Baldwin — son of the High Sheriff who had arrested him in 1451; he knew, too, that this Sir Baldwin when cheated out of his patrimony, "betook himself to a religious course of life . . . styling himself *Knight and Priest.*"

And then anon the hermit stanched Sir Launcelot's blood, and made him to drink good wine, so that he was well refreshed, and knew himself. For in those days it was not the guise of hermits as is nowadays. For there were none hermits in those days but that they had been men of Worship and of prowess, and those hermits held great household, and refreshed people that were in distress.

Nothing resembling this passage occurs in the source-books which Malory used. In the metrical *Morte Arthur* we are merely told that a leech healed Sir Launcelot's wounds, while the prose *Launcelot* says that an old knight of the neighbourhood, who knew much about surgery, was sent for. Malory's description of Sir Baudewin as "of Bretayne," [1] like his earlier statement that

---

[1] Sir E. Strachey's edition gives this as "Britanny" (meaning Brittany); but the spelling here adopted is that taken by Dr. Oskar Sommer from Caxton's copy.

Sir Melias de Lile was "son of the King of Denmark," must be regarded as proof of the large freedom he allowed himself. In this as in many other respects he shows how far he is from being merely a translator and collator of earlier contributions to the Arthurian Cycle.

That Sir Thomas Malory had in mind Guy's Cliffe, near Warwick, when he penned the following topographical details of Sir Baudewin's hermitage, is pretty certain. The passage occurs in Book XVIII of the *Morte*, and nothing corresponding to it is to be found in the prose *Launcelot* from which Malory derived the narrative.

Ever Sir Launcelot bled that it ran down to the earth. And so by fortune they came to that hermitage, which was under a wood, and a great cliff on the other side, and a fair water running under it.

This exactly describes the position of Guy's Cliffe, a place with which Malory would be well acquainted through his chief, Richard Beauchamp, Earl of Warwick. For it was here that, in 1423, the Earl founded a chantry, thus carrying into effect a wish expressed by Henry V on the occasion of a visit paid by the king to this hermitage, famous for its association with Guy of Warwick.

We come now to what is perhaps the most conclusive piece of *internal* evidence that Sir Thomas Malory, Knight, of Newbold Revel, wrote the *Morte d'Arthur*. If we think of the author as being detained in prison when a general amnesty is declared, we shall understand for the first time what he meant when he closed his work a year later with a request to all readers: "Pray for me, while I am on live that God send me good deliverance." And light will be cast on a passage concerning Sir Tristram, "who endured great pain" in captivity, "for sickness had overtaken him, and that is the greatest pain a prisoner may have. For all the while a prisoner may have his health of body he may endure under the mercy of God and in hope of good deliverance; but when sickness touches a prisoner's body, then may a prisoner say all wealth is him bereft, and then he hath cause to wail and to weep."

Very seldom does Malory indulge in reflections not to be found in the original romances from which he worked. This is one of those rare passages; and it is natural to see in it the impelling force of bitter personal experience. We may take it, then, that — like certain of St. Paul's Epistles, the *Pilgrim's Progress*, and Raleigh's *History of the World* — the *Morte d'Arthur* was written in captivity.

The world is more indebted than is commonly supposed to prisons for outstanding works of Literature. Boethius, Lovelace, Wilde, and Ernst Toller are some of the names which may be noted in this connection. English prisons of the present day are vastly superior to old Newgate from a sanitary point of view, — although it should be remembered that a water supply was provided for Newgate by Lord Mayor Richard Whittington, — but since the Bottomley episode it is very doubtful whether a gaol in this country is a favourable place for literary endeavour.

Chapter XVI

MALORY'S PROSE STYLE

HAD Malory been permitted to pass his life on his manor of Newbold Revel, it is exceedingly unlikely that he would have had access to the manuscript books which were necessary to him in compiling the *Morte*. This, it must be remembered, was fused into its actual form out of crude materials ten times greater in bulk. When Malory began his task, the best of the Arthurian romances were still in French. But cultivated England was now following Chaucer's lead and ceasing to talk French; and Malory — with Wycliffe's example before him — would have no doubt as to what language would henceforth hold sway in England.

It should here be noted how prominently the Midlands were represented in this nationalist reaction. Layamon and Walter Langland are household words to us; and Lawrence Minot, who flourished exactly a century before Malory and whose dialect in his ballads proclaims him a Midlander, is the first to give literary expression to the protest against our native language falling to obscure rank and menial uses. It is worth noting, too, as a coincidence, that the fourteenth-century metrical *Morte Arthur* (one of the source-books used by Malory) has been definitely assigned to "the Northern border of the West Midland region" — precisely that part of England in which Sir Thomas spent his early days.

Warwickshire has always been noted for sport, and that Sir Thomas Malory was a sportsman through and through we may conclude from his original and carefully drawn picture of Sir Tristram.

Every day Sir Tristram would go ride on hunting, for Sir Tristram was, that time called the best chaser of the world, and the noblest blower of an horn of all manner of measures. For, as books report, of Sir Tristram came all the good terms of venery and hunting, and all the sizes and measures of blowing of an horn; and of him we had first all the terms of hawking, and which were beasts of chase, and beasts of venery, and which were vermins; and all the blasts that belong to all manner of games.

Sir Thomas Malory, too, had a genuine Warwickshire man's regard for horses. On the occasion of one of the innumerable tournaments spoken of in the *Morte* we are told:

Then was the cry huge and great when Sir Palamides the Saracen smote the neck of Sir Launcelot's horse that it died. For many knights held that it was unknightly done in tournament to kill a horse wilfully — except it were done in plain battle, life for life.

In spite of the bloodshed and the other features which Roger Ascham condemned in the *Morte*, we do get the vision of a really "Merrie England" when reading Malory's pages. On one occasion, we read, King Arthur and Launcelot "laughed that they might not sit"; and when Guinevere sees poor Sir Dinadan after a bout with Launcelot (he having been despoiled unto his shirt and a woman's garment put upon him) "then the Queen laughed that she fell down, and so did all that were there."

How picturesque, too, is the way in which Malory closes his account of a day's sport: "And then the King let blow to lodging." How much more full of life than our phrases: "Hounds then returned to kennels," or "Home was then the order."

Sir Thomas Malory, surely, was a sportsman in another very different matter — his treatment of Guinevere's character. Some earlier writers on the theme of Launcelot and Guinevere had inferred that the origin of all the trouble was to be found on the Queen's side, — "The woman, she tempted me," — but Sir Thomas will not stoop to this. "While she lived," he contents himself with saying of Guinevere, "she was a true lover, and therefore she had a good end."

Take another example of Malory's prose, which should be prefaced by recalling that on one occasion the knights of the Round Table are subjected to a test — the curing of the wounds of Sir Urre of Hungary, who should never be made whole until the best knight in the world had probed his wounds. One after the other, King Arthur's paladins fail to achieve the miracle, until at last it is Launcelot's turn to try his hand. Conscious of his sin with Guinevere, he shrinks from the ordeal, but is ordered by the King to proceed:

Then Sir Launcelot kneeled down by the wounded knight, saying, My lord Arthur, I must do your commandment, the which is sore against my heart. And then he held up his hands, and looked into the east, saying secretly unto himself, Thou blessed Father, Son, and Holy Ghost, I beseech thee of thy mercy, that my simple worship and honesty be saved, and thou, blessed Trinity, thou mayest give power to heal this sick knight, by thy great virtue and grace of thee, but, good Lord, never of myself. And then Sir Launcelot prayed Sir Urre to let him see his head: and then, devoutly kneeling, he ransacked the three wounds, that they bled a little, and forth with all the wounds fair healed, and seemed as they had

been whole a seven year. And in likewise he searched his
body of other three wounds, and they healed in likewise.
And then the last of all he searched the which was in his
hand, and, anon, it healed fair. Then King Arthur, and all the
kings and knights, kneeled down, and gave thanks and lov-
ings unto God, and to his blessed mother, and ever Sir Launcelot wept as he had been a child that had been beaten.

Judging from the *Morte*, it would seem that Malory
accepted the doctrine of Transubstantiation as readily
as did the average Lollard.[1] In Book XVII Malory says:

Then took he himself the holy vessel, and came to Galahad,
and he kneeled down and there he received his Saviour, and
after him so received all his fellows; and they thought it so
sweet that it was marvellous to tell.

Let us quote Professor Saintsbury: "It is possible
that Malory's art is mostly unconscious art — it is not
much the worse for that. But it is nearly as infallible
as it is either unconscious or thoroughly concealed. The
pictorial power, the musical cadence of the phrase, the
steady glow of chivalrous feeling throughout, the noble
morality (for the condemnation of Ascham and others
is partly mere Renaissance priggishness stupidly con-
demning things mediæval off-hand, and partly Puritan
prudery throwing its baleful shadow before), the kindli-
ness, the sense of honour, the melancholy and yet never
either gloomy or puling sense of the inevitable end —
all these are eminent in it." No effort in English prose
on so large a scale had been made before Malory, and
he did much to encourage a fluent and pliant English
prose style in the century that succeeded him.

[1] "The Lollards never devised a new sacrament of their own, . . . and
there is no suggestion in Lollard literature that they repudiated the obliga-
tion to hear Mass on Sunday and holy days." — M. Deanesley, *The Lollard
Bible.*

We may agree with Professor Saintsbury that "The thing is important in Literature, not the man"; but in studying what is known of the knight of Newbold Revel we gain a better conception of a work which a competent critic has declared to be "not only the greatest of English prose romances, but also in a very real sense the pioneer of the English Novel." If, as Robert Louis Stevenson has so finely said, "a man would rather leave behind him the portrait of his spirit than the portrait of his face, — *figura animi magis quam corporis*," — then Sir Thomas Malory may rest well satisfied. "In audacitie forward," he is shaped after the pattern of Sir Launcelot de Lake, whose knightly exploits and human failings are depicted so faithfully in the *Morte*.

Four and a half centuries have passed since Caxton "enprised" to print Malory's "book of the noble histories of King Arthur," with its lesson so plainly written—

Do after the good and leave the evil, and it shall bring you to good fame and renommée.

Successive generations have approved the wisdom of Caxton's choice. If we regard Malory as in some measure typifying Sir Launcelot, we shall agree that, like him, he has received double for all his sins.

APPENDICES

APPENDIX I

THE TRIAL OF SIR THOMAS MALORY

INQUISITION AT NUNEATON.

KING'S BENCH INDICTMENTS. File 265, Bundle 38. Supplemented from Coram Rege Roll 763 m 3 Crown Side. Hilary Term, 30 Hen. VI.

Inquisitio capta apud Nuneton coram Humfrido Duce Buk. Willelmo Birmyngeham milite, Thoma Bate & Thoma Greswold Custodibus pacis domini Regis Ac Justiciariis ipsius domini Regis ad diversas felonias, transgressiones, & malefactas in Comitatu Warr. audiendum & terminandum assignatis die lune proximo ante festum sancti Bartholome Apostoli Anno regni Regis Henrici sexti post conquestum vicesimo nono per sacramentum Ricardi Arblaster de Birmyngeham, Johannis Belle de eadem, Johannis Whatcroft de Solyhull, Rogeri More de eadem, — Corpeson de Bykenhull, Thome Dounton de Sheldon, Alani Gervys de Merston Culy, Ricardi Orme de eadem, Thome Mylner de Atherston, Ricardi Barbour de eadem, Henrici Blakenhale de Sheldon, Willelmi Parker de Atherston, Willelmi Vale de eadem, Willelmi Ludford de Austeley & Henrici Serche de Hurley qui dicunt super sacramentum suum quod cum Humfridus Dux Buk., virtute cuiusdem Commissionis domini Regis eidem Duci Ac Ricardo Comiti Warr. directi ad capiendum & arestandum Thomam Malory nuper de Fenny Newbold in Comitatu Warr. militem & Johannem Appelby servientem eiusdem Thome pretextu cuiusquidem commissionis Idem Dux die dominica in festa Sancti Jacobi Apostoli Anno regni Regis Henrici sexti post conquestum vicesimo nono apud Fenny Newbold dictum Thomam Malory capit [cepit?] & arrestavit & ipsum apud Coventre, Willelmo Mountfort militi vicecomiti Comitatus Warr. comisit ad ipsum Thomam salvo & secure custodien-

dum. Ita quod posset habere corpus eiusdem Thome coram
domino Rege & concilo suo in quindena sancti Michaelis
proxima future ubicumque tunc foret in Anglia ad respon-
dendum eidem domino Regi de & super diversis articulis in
eadem Commissione specificatis necnon faciendum & reci-
piendum que tunc de concilio predicto contingerit ordinari.
Super quo dictus Thomas die Martis extunc proximo sequente
in prisona sub custodia dicti vicecomitis apud Colshull in
manerio ibidem prisonam predictam in nocte dicte die Martis
noctanter fregit & ultra motam ibidem natavit sicque a custodia dicti vicecomitis evasit. Ac tunc dictus Thomas, Johannes Appleby nuper de Fenny Newbold in Comitatu Warr.
Gentilman, Johannes Sherd nuper de eisdem villa & Comitatu
yoman, ... Willelmus Halle nuper de Stonley in Comitatu predicto yoman, Johannes Masshot nuper de Fenny
Newbold in Comitatu predicto Grome, ... Rogerus Sherd
nuper de eisdem villa & Comitatu yoman, Thomas Sherd
nuper de eisdem villa & Comitatu yoman, Johannes Tynock
nuper de Wolvey in comitatu predicto husbondman, Gregorius Walshale de Brynkelow in Comitatu predicto yoman,
Ricardus Irysshman nuper de Fenny Newbold in Comitatu
predicto laborer & Thomas Maryot nuper de Kyrkeby Monachorum in Comitatu predicto yoman, aggregatis sibi quampluribus malefactoribus & pacis domini Regis perturbatoribus
ignotis ut rebelles ac pacis domini Regis perturbatores modo
nove insurrexionis unanimiterque insurrexerunt & die Mer-
curii ex tunc proximo sequente ad Monasterium & Abbatiam
beate Marie de Combe perrexerunt & diversas portas & ostia
eiusdem Monasterii cum magnis lignis noctanter fregerunt &
intraverunt & duas cistas Abbatis dicti Monasterii adtunc &
ibidem fregerunt & una bagam & viginti & una libras auri in
eadem contentas & una aliam bagam & viginti & quinque
marcas auri & argenti in eadem baga contentas de bonis &
catallis dicti Abbatis & Conventus ibidem ac quamplura alia
jocalia & ornamenta ecclesie dicti Monasterii et Abbatis ad
valenciam quadraginta librarum adtunc & ibidem inventa
felonice ceperunt & asportaverunt in magnam destructionem
& spoliacionem Monasterii & Abbatie predicte necnon contra
pacem coronam & dignitatem domini Regis.

Item dicunt quod Thomas Malory nuper de Fenny Newbold in Comitatu Warr. Miles ac quamplures alii malefactores
& pacis domini Regis perturbatores ignoti ad numerum viginti
& sex personarum armatarum & modo guerrino arraiatarim
videlicet gladiis, baculis, gleyves, arcubus, sagittis, Jakkes,
Salettes & crossebowes quarto die Januarii Anno regni Regis
Henrici sexti post conquestum vicesimo octavo apud Combe
in Silvis Abbatis beate Marie de Combe predicta jacuerunt
in insidiis ad interficiendum & murdrum Humfridum Ducem
Buk. & ad ipsum cum arcubus & sagittis predictis sagittan-
dum & interficiendum contra pacem dicti domini Regis.

Item dicunt quod Thomas Malory nuper de Fenneneubold
in Comitatu Warr. Miles, Ricardus Malory de Radclyff juxta
Leycestre in Comitatu Leyc. Armiger, Johannes Appulby de
Fenneneubold in Comitatu Warr. Gentilman, Johannes Sherd
nuper de Fenneneubold in Comitatu Warr yoman alias dictus
Johannes Shoo de Fenneneubold in Comitatu Warr. yoman,
Willelmus Podmore nuper de Fenneneubold in Comitatu
Warr. yoman, Willelmus Halle nuper de Stonley in Comitatu
Warr. Walker, Johannes Masshot nuper de Fenneneubold in
Comitatu Warr. Grome, Rogerus Sherd nuper de Fenneneu-
bold in Comitatu Warr. yoman, alias dictus Thomas Shoo
nuper de Fenneneubold in Comitatu Warr. yoman . . . . in
Comitatu Warr husbondman, Gregorius Walshale nuper de
Brynkelowe in Comitatu Warr . . . Brynkelow in Comitatu
Warr. husbondman, Ricardus Irysshman nuper de Fenneneu-
bold in . . . nuper de Kyrkeby Monachorum in Comitatu
Warr. Bower, Thomas Leghton nuper de . . . Robertus
Smyth nuper de Fenneneubold in Comitatu Warr. Smyth,
Johannes Warr . . . yoman, Johannes Harper nuper de
Fenneneubold in Comitatu Warr. harper, et Johannes . . .
Cook, die Jovis proximo post festum sancti Jacobi Apostoli
Anno regni Regis Henrici sexti post conquestum vicesimo
nono supradicto aggregatis sibi quampluribus malefactoribus
et pacis domini Regis perturbatoribus ignotis ad numerum
Centum personarum modo guerrino arraiatarum vi et armis
videlicet, gladiis, lanciis, lassinis, arcubus, & sagittis clausa &
domos Ricardi Abbatis Monasterii beate Marie de Comba

apud Combe in Comitatu Warr. modo riote intraverunt &
octodecim ostia monasterii predicti fregerunt & in predictum
Ricardum Abbatem, commonachos & servientes suos adtunc
& ibidem insultam fecerunt & tres citas ferro ligatas & ceratas
violenter fregerunt & quadraginta libras quatuor solidos &
quatuor denarios in pecunia munerata in diversis bagis contentas & tres annulos auri cum lapidibus preciosis precii
Centum solidorum & due signeta argenti precii sex solidorum
& octo denariorum unum parvum psalterum precii vjs viijd
duas zonas argenti precii xxxs tria paria preculum videlicet
"bedes" unum parum de Corall precii vs alterum de laumbir
precii vs tercium de Jete precii duorum solidorum duos arcus
precii vs & tres garbas de sagittis precii vjs de bonis & catallis
predicti Abbatis ibidem inventis felonice furati fuerunt.

Item dicunt quod Thomas Malory nuper de Fenny New-
bold in Comitatu Warr. Miles & Johannes . . . in eodem
Comitatu Gentilman ultimo die Augusti Anno regni Regis
Henrici Sexti post conquestum vicesimo octavo apud Mon-
keskirkeby per minas & oppressionem ceperunt extorciose de
Johanne Mylner viginti solidos. Iidem Thomas Malory &
Johannes Appelby ultimo die Maii Anno regni Regis Henrici
sexti . . . vicesimo octavo apud Monkeskyrkeby predictam
extorciose ceperunt per minas & oppressionem de Margareta
Kyng & Willelmo Hale Centum solidos.

Item dicunt quod Thomas Malory nuper de Fenny Newbold in Comitatu Warr. Miles die sabati proximo ante festum
Pentecostes Anno regni Regis Henrici sexti post conquestum vicesimo octavo apud Kirkeby Monachorum clausum &
domos Hugonis Smyth fregit & Johannam uxorem dicti Hugonis ibidem adtunc felonice rapuit & cum ea carnaliter
concubuit.

Item dicunt quod Thomas Malory nuper de Fenny Newbold in Comitatu Warr. Miles die Jovis proximo post festum
Sancti Petri Advincula Anno regni Regis Henrici sexti post
conquestum vicesimo octavo Johannam uxorem Hugonis
Smyth apud Coventre felonice rapuit & cum ea carnaliter
concubuit. Ac illam cum bonis & catallis dicto Hugonis ad

valenciam quadraginta librarum tunc & ibidem inventis
usque Barwell in Comitatu Leyc. felonice furatis fuit cepit &
abduxit contra pacem coronam & dignitatem domini Regis.

Item alias Inquisitio capta coram prefatis Justiciariis die
loco & Anno supradictis per sacramentum Willelmi . . .
Dunchurche, Ricardi Gebons de Ulfreton, Johannis Bynley
de Rokeby, Willelmi . . . Thome Halle de Lalleford, Johannis Bemonde de Bromkote, Johannis Herdw . . . Saun-
dres de Bedworth, Johannis Faukes de Radford Symly,
Willelmi . . . Thomas Malory de Fenny Newbold in Comitatu Warr. Miles, Johannes Mas . . . , Willelmus Smyth
de eisdem villa & Comitatu laborer, Galfridus Gryffyn de
. . . Carleton in Comitatu Leycestr yoman & Johannes
Arnesby de Ty . . . quarto die Junii Anno regni Regis
Henrici sexti post conquestum vicesimo nono apud Cosford
septem vaccas duos boviculos trescentas triginta & quinque
oves precii xxijl*i* & una carecta cum ferro ligata precii iiijl*i*
de bonis & catallis Willelmi Rowe & Willelmi Dowde de
Shatewell in Comitatu Leyc. extorcione ceperunt & abinde
usque Newbold abduxerunt contra pacem domini Regis etc.

BEFORE THE KING'S BENCH.

[Continued from Coram Rege Roll 763 Crown Side Membrane 3.]

Quequidem judicamenta dominus Rex nunc coram eo
postea certis de causis venire fecit terminanda. Propter quod
preceptum fuit vicecomiti quod non omittet ac quin caperet
eos si &c. Et modo scilicet die Jovis in quindena Sancti Hillarii isto eodem termino coram domino Rege apud Westmonasterium venit predictus Thomas Malory per vicecomites
London virtute brevis domini Regis eis inde directi ad baram
hic ductus in propria persona sua et statim de premissis sibi
superius impositus allocutus qualiter se velit inde acquietare
dicit quod ipse in nullo est inde culpabilis. Et inde de bono &
malo ponit se super patriam &c. Et super hoc idem Thomas
Malory remittitur prefatis vicecomitibus predictis salvo
custodiendis quousque &c. una cum causis &c.[1]

---

[1] In margin: "Remittitur London."

[Added later.]

Et in hac parte venit inde jurata coram domino Rege in
octavo Purificationis beate Marie ubicumque &c. Et qui &c.
ad recognoscendum &c. Quia &c. Idem dies datum est prefato Thome Malory &c. Ad quem diem coram domino Rege
apud Westmonasterium venit predictus Thomas Malory sub
custodia prefatorum Vicecomitum in propria persona. Et
Vicecomites retornant nomina xxiiij Juratorum quorum nullas
&c. Ita preceptum est Vicecomitibus quod non ommittant
&c. quin distringant eos per mones terras &c. Et quod de
exitibus &c. Et quod habeant corpora eorum coram domino
Rege a die Pasche in xv dies ubicumque &c. ad faciendum
Juratam predictam &c. Et quod apponant xx tales &c. Idem
dies datum est prefato Thome Malory in custodia prefatorum
Vicecomitum interim commissio &c. postea scilicet a die
Pasche in xv dies Anno regni dicti Regis tricesimo secundo
coram ipso Rege apud Westmonasterium venit predictus
Thomas Malory in propria persona sua. Et Vicomites non
nunc inde littere &c.

Preceptum est vicecomitibus quod non ommittant &c quin
distringant juratores dicte jurate per omnes terras &c et quod
de exitibus &c et quod habeant corpora eorum coram domino
Rege a die sancti Michaelis in unum mensem ubicumque &c.
Nisi dilectus & fidelis domini Regis Ricardus Byngham unius
justicarius dicti Regis ad plactium &c prius die Jovis proximo
ante festum sancti Matthei apostoli apud Warrewyk per
formam statuti &c venerit ad faciendum juratam predictam.
Idem dies datum est prefato Thome Malory. Et super hoc de
gratia Curie speciali predictus Thomas Malory dimittitur per
manucaptionem Rogeri Chamberleyn de Quynburgh in
Comitatu Kanc. militis, Johannis Leventhorpe de London
armigeris, Edwardi Fitz William de Framlyngham in Comitatu Suff. armigeris, Thome Ince de Comitatu Essex armigeris, Radulphi Worthyngton de Framlyngham in Comitatu
Suff. Gentilman, Edwardi Wheteley de London Gentleman
& Johannis Hathwyk de Herbury in Comitatu Warr. Gentilman qui eam inquisitionem habendi corporis eius coram domino Rege ad prefatum terminum &c. Postea scilicet die

Veneris proximo post xvam Sancti Hillarii Anno regni dicti
Regis tricesimo quarto coram ipso Rege apud Westmonasterium venit predictus Thomas Malory sub custodia Thome
Gower Armigeris locumtenentis Henrici Ducis Exonie Con-
stabularii domini Regis Turris sui London virtute brevis dicti
Regis eisdem Constabulario & locum tenenti inde directi in
propria persona sua. Qui comittitur Marescallo &c et cum
hoc idem Thomas Malory quod dominus Rex nunc de gratia
sua speciali & ex certa sciencia & mero motu suis post ultimam
contumacionem placiti predicti scilicet xvam sancti Michaelis
termino proximam precedentem per litteras suas patentes
pardonavit remisit & relaxavit eidem Thome quouscumque
nomine censedatur secta pacis sue que ad ipsum Regem versus
ipsum Thomam pertinet pro felonis, transgressionibus, insur-
rectionibus, extortionibus, oppressionibus & aliis offensis
predictis & pro omnibus aliis feloniis & transgressionibus per
ipsum Thomam ante novum diem Julii Anno regni dicti Regis
tricesimo tercio factis sive perpetratis et firmam pacem suam
ei inde concessit. Et profert hic in Curiam litteras patentes
predictas premissa testificantes quarum datum est apud
Westmonasterium vicesimo quarto die Novembris Anno regni
dicti Regis tricesimo quarto supradicto. Et super venit
Rogerus Malory de Ryton in Comitatu Warr. Gentilman,
Johannes Benford de London Gentilman, Willelmus Clyff
de London Gentilman, Walterus Boys de London Sadeler,
Thomas Pulton de London Taillour & David John de London
Taillour de manucaptione pro prefato Thoma Malory quod
ipse extunc se bene geret erga dominum Regem in & cunctum
populum suum juxta formam statuti in huiusmodo casu editi
& provisi. Quarum Litterarum domini Regis patencium ac
manucaptionis predicte predictus Thomas Malory petit quod
ipse de premissis per Curiam hic dimittatur &c Super quo visis
premissis Consideratum est quod idem Thomas Malory eat
inde sine die &c. et quod Juratores dicte Jurate in hac parte
exonerentur &c et predictus Thomas Malory remaneat in
custodia prefati Marescalli pro sufficienti securitati pacis erga
dominum Regem & cunctum populum suum inveniendo
quousque &c.

K.B. Coram Rege Roll 778 Rex m 34 Hil. 34 Hen. VI.
Warr.

Juratores ad recognoscendum &c. Si Thomas Malory nuper
de Fenny Newbolde in Comitatu predicto Miles alias dictus
Thomas Malory de Fenny Newbold in Comitatu predicto
Miles culpabilis sit de diversis feloniis, transgressionibus, in-
surreccionibus extortionibus unde indicatus est necne ponitur
in respicium coram domino Rege usque a die Sancti Hillarie
in xv dies ubicumque &c pro defectu Juratorum &c. Ideo
Vicecomes habeat corpora &c. Idem dies datus prefato
Thome &c. Et sciendum est quod littere inde deliberantur
hic in curia Willelmo Coton deputato Willelmi Hastynges
Armirgei Vicecomitis Comitatus predicti die Sabati proximo
post xviija Scancti Martini isto eodem termino ad exequendas
&c.

K.B. Controlment Roll 87 Michs. 36 Hen. VI m 17.
London.

Thomas Malory nuper de Fenny Newbold in Comitatu
Warr. Miles per Willelmum Edward & Thomam Reyner
Vicomites Londonie virtute brevis domini Regis de habeas
corpus eis directi coram Rege ductus cum causa videlicet,
quod idem Thomas commissis fuit prisone domini Regis in
Civitate Londonie per Johannem Fortescu Militem Capi-
talem Justiciarum domini Regis pro diversis causis coram
domino Rege pendentibus & pro eo similiter quod ipse cuidem
Thome Greswold condempnatus existit. Et idem Thomas
Malory detentus est interim in prisona predicta pretextu
cuiusdam alterius brevis domini Regis cuius tenor sequitur in
hec verba — Henricus Dei gratia Rex Anglie, Francie &
dominus Hibernie Vicomitibus Londonie Salutem. Quia
Thomas Malory Miles in prisona nostra Marescalcie nostre
coram nobis pro securitate pacis nostre erga nos & cunctum
populum nostrum & percipue erga Abbatem de Combe &
plures alios de ligeis nostris ac pro securitate de se bene
gerendo erga nos & cunctum populum nostrum invenienda
& aliis certis de causis nos specialiter moventibus detentus
exitit. Nos pro maiore securitate custodie prefati Thome
ipsum Thomam nuper vicecomiti nostro Middlesex com-

miserimus in prisona nostra de Neugate sub custodia ipsius nuper vicecomitis salvo & secure excausis predictis custodiendum quousque aliud de eo ordinaverimus & hoc sub pena milla librarum nullatenus omitteret. Jamque pro eo quod predictus in Curia nostra coram nobis acceperimis quod predictus Thomas in prisona nostra de Ludgate sub custodia vostra ex causis predictis modo existit detentus vobis precipimus firmiter injungentes quod predictum Thomam in prisona nostra salvo & secure ex causis predictis custodiatis sub pena supradicta quousque aliud a nobis inde habuertis in mandatis. Teste J Fortescu apud Westmonasterium xxiiij die Januarie Anno regni nostri tricesimo quinto. Qui commitatur Marescalcie &c.

[*Added later.*]

Postea die mercurie proximo post xviiia Sancti Michaelis isto termino predictus Thomas Malory traditur in ballivum Willelmo Nevyle domino de Fauconberge, Willelmo Briggeham de Briggeham in Comitatu Eboracie Armigero & Johanni Clerkson de Arundell in Comitatu Sussex armigero usque crastina [Sancti] Johannis ubicumque &c. quilibet plegiarius sub pena xxl*i* & predictus Thomas Malory sub pena ccccl*i* sub r [?] &c. Ac de bono gestu suo &c. Ad quem diem comparuit & commititur Marescallo tam pro securitate pacis predicte quam de bono gestu suo &c. Aceciam pro condempnatione predicte &c.

[*Added later.*]

Postea scilicet termino pasche anno regni dicti Regis tricesimo septimo pro eo quod informatur curia hic per fidedignos Comitatus Warr. quod dictus Thomas extra custodiam dicti Marescalli fuit in dicto comitatu Warr. ad largum post festum Pasche dicto termino tricesimo septimo dictum [?] est hic per curiam prefato Marescallo quod idem Marescallus prefatum Thomam Malory in prisona domini Regis Marescallcie domini Regis apud Suthwerk in Comitatu Surrie custodire faceret & non ad largum . . . permittit ipsum Thomam extra prisonam [decetero ire] & hoc sub penam centum librarum &c.

[Added later.]

Et postea scilicet termino Sancti Hillari Anno regni dicti
Regis tricesimo octavo predictus Thomas Malory comittitur
custodie vicomitis Middlesex pro causis predictis in prisona
domini Regis de Nugate salvo & secure moraturi quousque
&c. Ideo dictus Marescallus de eo hic exoneratur &c.

[TRANSLATION.]

Inquisition taken at Noneton [Nuneaton] before Humfrey,
Duke of Buckingham, William Birmyngham Knt., Thomas
Bate and Thomas Greswold, Keepers of the Peace (Custodibus Pacis) of the lord the King and Justices of the same lord
the King, assigned to hear and determine divers felonies,
transgressions and misdeeds in the County of Warwick on
Monday next before the feast of St. Bartholomew the Apostle
in the twenty-ninth year of the reign of King Henry the sixth
since the Conquest, by the oaths of Richard Ablaster of
Birmyngham, John Belle of the same, John Whatcroft of
Solyhull, Roger More of the same, —— Corpeson of Bykenhull, Thomas Dounton of Seldon, Alan Gervys of Mers-
ton-Culy, Richard Orme of the same, Thomas Mylner of
Atherston, Richard Barbour of the same, Henry Blakenhale
of Sheldon, William Parker of Ath[ers]ton, William Vale of
of the same, William Ludford of Austerley, and Henry Serche
of Hurley, who say on their oath that Humfrey Duke of
Buckingham by virtue of certain commissions of our lord the
King directed to the same Duke and Richard, Earl of Warwick, to take and arrest Thomas Malory late of Fenny Newbold in County Warwick, Knight, and John Appelby, servant
of the same Thomas, by authority of such commissions, on
Sunday in the feast of St. James the Apostle in the twenty-
ninth year of King Henry the sixth after the Conquest, at
Fenny Newbold took and arrested the said Thomas Malory,
and at Coventry committed the same to William Mountford
Knt. Sheriff of the County of Warwick to keep the same
Thomas safe and secure, so that he might have the body of
the same Thomas before the lord the King and his Councell
in the quinden [fifteen days] of St. Michael next ensuing

wheresoever he might then be in England. To answer to the same lord the King of and upon divers articles in the same commission specified as well as to do and receive what shall then be ordered by the Councell aforesaid.

Upon which the said Thomas on Tuesday then next following under the custody of the said Sheriff in prison in the manor of Colshull [Coleshill], broke out of the aforesaid prison in the night of the aforesaid Tuesday and swam across the moat there thus evading the custody of the said Sheriff. And then the said Thomas Malory and John Appelby late of Fenny Newbold in the County of Warwick, Gentleman, John Sherd late of the same town and county yoman, . . . William Halle late of Stonley in the aforesaid county, yoman, John Masshot late of Fenny Newbold in the same county, grome, Roger Sherd late of the same town and county, yoman, Thomas Sherd late of the same town and county, yoman, John Tyncok late of Wolvey in the county aforesaid, husbondman, Gregory Walshal of Brynkelowe in the county aforesaid, yoman, Richard Irysshman late of the said Fenny Newbold in the aforesaid county, laborer, and Thomas Maryot late of Monks Kyrkeby in the county aforesaid, assembled with many other malefactors and breakers of the King's peace unknown, as rebels and breakers of the King's peace in the manner of an insurrection, unanimously rose, and on Wednesday then next following broke into the Monastery and Abbey of Blessed Mary of Combe and with great baulks of wood by night broke and entered divers gates and doors of the same monastery and there and then broke into two chests of the Abbot of the same monastery and one bag containing twenty-one pounds of gold and another bag containing twenty-five gold and silver marks of the goods and chattels of the said Abbot and Convent and many other jewels and ornaments of the church of the said monastery and abbey to the value of forty pounds then and there feloniously took and carried away in great destruction and spoiliation of the monastery and abbey aforesaid as well as against the peace of our lord the King, his crown and dignity.

Item, they say that Thomas Malory late of Fenny Newbold in the county of Warwick, Knight, and many other male-

factors and breakers of the King's peace unknown, to the
number of twenty-six persons, armed and arrayed in warlike
manner, namely, with swords, staves, glaives, bows, arrows,
Jakkes, Salettes, crossebowes, on the fourth day of January
in the twenty-eighth year of the reign of King Henry the sixth
after the Conquest at Combe, in the woods of the Abbey of
Blessed Mary of Combe aforesaid, lay in ambush to kill and
murder Humfrey, Duke of Buckingham, and the same with
the bows and arrows aforesaid to shoot and kill, against the
peace of the said lord the King.

Item, they say that Thomas Malory, late of Fenny New-
bold in the county of Warwick, Knt., Richard Malory, of
Radclyff-next-Leycestre, in county Leicester, Esq., John Ap-
pulby late of Fenneneubold in county Warwick, Gentilman,
John Sherd late of Fenenewbold &c., yoman, otherwise John
Shoo . . . Fenenneubold, &c., William Podmore late of
Fenneubold &c. yoman, William Hall, late of Stonley in
county Warwick, walker [fuller], John Masshot late of Fenneneubold in county Warwick, grome, Roger Sherd late of
Fenneneubold in county Warwick, yoman, otherwise Roger
Shoo late of, &c., Thomas Sherd late of Fenneneubold in
county Warwick, yoman, otherwise Thomas Shoo, late of &c.
. . . county of Warwick, husbondman, Gregery Walshale,
late of Brinkelowe in county Warwick . . . Brynkelowe in
the county of Warwick, husbondman, Richard Irysshman
late of Fenneneubold in . . . late of Monks Kyrkeby in the
county of Warwick, bower, Thomas Leghton late of . . .
Robert Smyth late of Fenneneubold in the county of Warwick, smyth, John Warr . . . Warwick, yoman, John Harper
late of Fenneneubold in the county of Warwick, harper, John
. . . , cook, on Thursday next after the feast of St. James the
Apostle in the abovesaid twenty-ninth year of the reign of
King Henry the sixth after the Conquest assembled with
many other malefactors and breakers of the King's peace
unknown to the number of a hundred persons arrayed in warlike manner with force and arms, namely with swords, lances,
ropes, bows and arrows, entered the close and house of Richard, Abbott of the monastery of Blessed Mary of Combe at

Combe in the county of Warwick in a riotous manner and broke eighteen doors of the aforesaid monastery, and then and there insulted the aforesaid Richard, the Abbot, his monks and servants and violently broke open three iron chests corded and sealed and forty pounds four shillings and fourpence in money found in divers bags and three gold rings with precious stones worth a hundred shillings and two silver signets worth six shillings and eightpence and one pair of psalters worth six shillings and eightpence two silver zones worth thirty shillings, three pairs of "preculum" — namely "bedes," one pair coral worth five shillings, another of "laumber" worth five shillings, and the third of "Jete" worth two shillings — two bows worth five shillings and three sheaves of arrowes worth six shillings of the goods and chattels of the aforesaid Abbot there found were feloniously stolen.

Item, they say that Thomas Malory late of Fenny Newbold in the county of Warwick, Knight, and John [Appelby] in the same county, gentilman, on the last day of August in the said twenty-eighth year of the reign of King Henry the sixth after the Conquest at Monkeskirkeby by threats and oppression took extortionately from John Mylner twenty shillings; and that the same Thomas Malory and John Appelby on the last day of May in the aforesaid twenty-eighth year &c. at Monkeskyrkeby aforesaid extortionately took by threats and oppression, a hundred shillings from Margaret Kyng and William Hales.

Item, they say that Thomas Malory late of Fenny Newbold in the county of Warwick, Knight, on Saturday next before the feast of Pentecost in the twenty-eighth year of the reign of King Henry the sixth after the Conquest, at Monks Kirkby broke into the close and house of Hugh Smyth, and Joan the wife of the said Hugh feloniously raped and lived carnally with.

Item, they say that Thomas Malory late of Fenny Newbold in the county of Warwick, Knight, on Thursday next after the feast of St. Peter-in-Chains in the twenty-eighth

year of the reign of King Henry the sixth &c. feloniously
raped Joan the wife of Hugh Smyth at Coventry and lived
carnally with the same. And that the goods and chattels of
the same Hugh to the value of forty pounds then and there
found he feloniously stole, took, and carried away to Barwell
in the county of Leycester against the peace of our lord the
King, his crown and dignity.

Item, another inquisition taken before the aforesaid Jus-
tices, the day, place, and year aforesaid, by the oath of Wil-
liam . . . of Dunchurch, Richard Gebons of Ulfreton, John
Bynley of Rokeby [Rugby], William . . . . Thomas Halle of
Lalleford, John Bemonde of Bromkote, John Herd . . . .
Saunders of Bedworth, John Faukes of Radford Symly, and
William . . . that Thomas Malory of Fenny Newbold in
the county of Warwick, Knight, John Mas[shot], William
Smyth of the same town and county, labourer, Geoffrey,
Gryffyn of . . . , . . . of Carleton in the county of Leycester, yoman, and John Arnesley of Ty[?Twycross] on the 4th
day of June in the said twenty-ninth year of the reign of
King Henry the sixth after the Conquest at Cosford in the
county of [Warwick] extortionately took seven cows, two
calves, a cart worth four pounds, and three hundred and
thirty-five sheep worth twenty-two pounds of the goods and
chattels of William Rowe and William Dowde of Shatwell in
the county of Leceyster and from thence carried them off to
Newbold, against the King's peace.

BEFORE THE KING'S BENCH.

The Indictment came before our lord the King to determine
after certain other causes. Wherefore it was ordered that the
Sheriff should not omit, etc., and that he should take the
same, etc. And now on Wednesday the 15th day of St. Hilary's Term the said Thomas Malory came before our lord the
King at Westminster, brought by the Sheriffs of London by
virtue of a writ of our lord the King directed to them that he
should be led to the bar there in his own person (*in propria
persona sua*). And having forthwith been asked, in reference

to what had gone before, if he desired to be acquitted of the premisses, he says that he is in no wise guilty thereof, and for good or ill puts himself upon his country, etc. And thereupon the said Thomas Malory was handed back to the Sheriffs for safe custody until, together with the other causes, etc. [A marginal note appears here: "Remittitur London." (Sent back to London).]

[Later notes added on the Coram Rege Roll.]

Ordered that Thomas Malory be distrained of all his goods. 2nd Feb. 30 Hen. VI.

32 Henry VI. By special grace of the Court, Thomas Malory was dismissed by the bail of Roger Chamberleynn of Quynburgh in the county of Kent, Knight, John Leventhorp of London Esq., Edward FitzWilliam of Framlyngham in the county of Suffolk Esq., Thomas Juce of the county of Essex Esq., Ralph Worthyngton of Franlyngham in the county of Suffolk Gentleman, Edward Whetely of London Gent., and John Hathwyk of Herbury in the county of Warwick Gent., who have mainprision of his body.

On Friday next after the 18th of St. Hilary, 34 Henry VI, Thomas Malory was in the Court committed to the custody of the Marshal. And there Thomas Malory proffered Letters Patent bearing date at Westminster the 24th of November 34 Henry VI by which the King had pardoned the said Thomas for all felonies and transgressions committed by him before the 9th July 33 Henry VI. And Roger Malory of Ryton, Warwickshire Gent., John Besford of London Gent., William Clyffe of London Gent., Walter Boys of London Sadler, Thomas Pulton of London Taillour and David John of London Taillour went bail for Thomas Malory that he would bear himself well towards the King and all people. And Thomas Malory remains in the custody of the Marshal until sufficient security be found.

[Here a marginal note (in Latin) appears: "Letters Patent allowed. *Sine die.*"]

APPENDIX II

Chanc. Inq. P.M. Edw. IV, File 75, No. 46.

Inquisition taken at Northampton in the county of Northampton on Tuesday in the Feast of St. James the Apostle in
the 20th year of the reign of King Edward the Fourth after
the Conquest before Thomas Haselwode Escheator of the
said lord the King in the county aforesaid, by virtue of a writ
of the lord the King to the same escheator directed and by
this inquisition made, by the oaths of John Fosbroke, Gentyl-
man, John Alyn of Grendon, John Sma . . . of Earles Barton,
Edward Berwyk of Whissheton, John Adam of Chadeston,
William Nell of Dodington Parva, Richard Ketull of Earles
Baton, John Smythe of Wollaston, Richard Julyan of Wen-
dlyngburgh, John Hayne of the same, Thomas North of the
same, Thomas Fysher of Dodyngton Magna, Thomas Bar-
nard of the same, William Chery of Tukone and William
Wythinale of the same. Who say on their oath that Elizabeth Malory, late the wife of Thomas Malory Knight in
the said writ named, was seized in her demesne as of free
hold for term of her life, the day on which she died, of one
messuage, one virgate of land with appurtenances in Wynwyke in the county aforesaid. Which certain messuage and
virgate of land with appurtenances is held of the King in chief
by Knight Service namely, in the fourth part of one knights
fee, as of the said King's Honour of Peverell. And they say
that the said messuage and land are worth yearly besides
deductions, xxs. And further the aforesaid Jurors say that
the reversion of the said messuage and lands discends to
Nicholas Malory as kinsman and heir of Thomas Malory late
husband of the said Elizabeth, namely, son of Robert, son of
the aforesaid Thomas and Elizabeth. And the aforesaid
Jurors say that the aforesaid Elizabeth died on the first day
of October last past. And that the aforesaid Nicholas Malory
is kinsman and next heir of the said Elizabeth, namely, son of
Robert, son of the aforesaid Thomas and Elizabeth. And the

aforesaid Jurors say that the aforesaid Nicholas Malory is aged fourtenn years and more. And besides the aforsaid Jurors say that the said Elizabeth was seized in her demesne as of free hold for term of her life, on the day she died, of the manner of Wynwyke with appurtenances in the county aforesaid the reversion of the said manor descends to the above-named Nicholas Malory as kinsman and heir of the aforesaid Thomas, namely, son of Robert son of the aforesaid Thomas. And they say of whom the aforesaid manor with appurtenances is held and by what service they do not know. And the said Jurors say that the aforesaid manor with appurtenances is worth x*li.* a year besides deductions and the said Elizabeth did not hold any more lands &c. in the county aforesaid of the said lord the King or of any other on the day she died. On testimony of which things the abovenamed escheator and aforesaid Jurors have alternatively placed their seals the day and year abovesaid.

Inquisition taken at Ruyton upon Dunnesmore in the county of Warwick on Thursday after the feast of St. James the Apostle in the 20th year of the reign of King Edward IV before William Bristowe Escheator of the said Lord the King in the county aforesaid, by virtue of a writ of the said lord the King of "diem clausit extremum" to the said Escheator directed, by this inquisition made, by the oaths of William Durant Gentilman Thomas Desert Gentilman, Nicholas Croke of Stokton, William Westley of Eythorp, Richard Gode of Stretton, John Thurkyll of the same, John Bynley of the same, Thomas Robyns of Brokhurst, John Smart of the same, Henry Carpenter, William Howet of Rokeby, John Bykley of the same, John Newcombe of Brynkelowe, John . . . of Palyington, Jurors. Who say on their oath that Elizabeth who was the wife of Thomas Malory Knight in the said writ named was seized, the day she died, in her demesne as of free hold for term of her life of the manor of Newbold Fenne otherwise called Newbold Ryvell with all its appurtenances in the county aforesaid with reversion therof, after the death of the said Elizabeth, to Nicholas Malory, kinsman and heir of the aforesaid Thomas Malory, namely, son of

Robert Malory, son of the aforesaid Thomas Malory Knight
and his heir. And they say that the said manor is held of
Richard, Duke of York and Norfolk and Anne his wife as of
right of the said Anne, daughter and heir of John late Duke
of Norfolk deceased, by the service of one knights fee. Which
Anne is under age and in the guardianship of the aforenamed
lord the King, and holds the said manor of the said lord the
King in chief by service of one knight's fee. The same Jurors
say that the said manor with appurtenances . . . besides
deductions, vj*li*. xiij*s*. viij*d*. And further the aforesaid
Jurors say that the said Elizabeth in the said writ named died
on the last day of September last past. And that the aforesaid Nicholas Malory is . . . and heir of the aforesaid Elizabeth namely a son of Robert, son of the aforesaid Thomas
Malory and Elizabeth and is aged xiij years and more. And
that the aforesaid Elizabeth in the said writ named did
not hold any more lands or tenements in the county . . .
of the lord the King nor of any other on the said day on
which she died. In witness of which things to this indented
inquisition as well the said Escheator as the aforesaid Jurors
have placed their seals. Given the day and . . . abovesaid.

Inquisition taken at Lutterworth in the county of Leicester
on Tuesday next after the feast of St. Anne in the 20th year
of the reign of King Edward the IV, before William Bristowe
Escheator of the said lord the King in the county aforesaid,
by virtue of a writ of the said lord the King of "diem clausit
extremum" to the same Escheator directed and by this inquisition made, by the oaths of William Wolman of Lutterworth, Robert Welyams of the same, Ralph Brakley of the
same, William Thorpe of Misterton, John Tebot of the same,
John Smyth of the same, Richard Hellowes of Walcott,
Thomas Chapman of the same, William Lastell of the same,
Thomas Wale of the same, John Campyon of the same, John
Carter, Thomas Hande of Shawell, William Tidman of Lutterworth, Robert Roberdes of Swynford, Thomas Mariot of
the same, John Gibbe of Swynford and Henry Sharpe of the
same, Jurors. Who say on their oath that Elizabeth who was
the wife of Thomas Malory Knight in the writ named was
seized, the day she died, in her demesne as of free hold for

term of her life of the manor of Swynnerford with appurtenances in the county aforesaid. And of one messuage and two
virgates of land with appurtenances in Stormefeld in the same
county, with reversion thereof . . . Elizabeth . . . Malory kinsman and heir of the said Thomas Malory namely, son
of Robert Malory son of the aforesaid Thomas Malory
Knight and his heir. And they say that the manor aforesaid
is worth in all issues besides deductions iiij marks a year. And
the said messuage and lands in Stormefield are worth in all
issues besides deductions xxvjs. viijd. yearly. But of whom
or by what service the manor, messuages and lands aforesaid
are held or any part of them is held the Jurors do not know.
And moreover the same Jurors say on their oaths that the
aforesaid Elizabeth in the said writ named died on the last
day of September last past. And that the aforesaid Nicholas
Malory is kinsman and heir of the aforesaid Elizabeth namely,
son of Robert son of the aforesaid Thomas Malory and Elizabeth and is aged xiij years and more. And that the aforenamed Elizabeth in the said writ named did not hold any
more lands or tenements in the county aforesaid of the lord
the King, or any other on the day she died, in the county
aforesaid. In witness of which things to this indented inquisition as well the abovenamed Escheator as the aforesaid
Jurors have placed their seals. Given the day and year
abovesaid.

INDEX

INDEX